8-95

Susan Stromberg-Stein

Louis Dudek

A Biographical Introduction to his Poetry

ISBN 0-919614-50-7

Printed and bound in Canada. ?~?~? METROLITHO INC. SHERBROOKE

The Golden Dog Press gratefully acknowledges the support accorded to its publishing programme by the Ontario Arts Council and the Canada Council.

20th anniversary
20ᵉ anniversaire
1963-1983

Canadian Cataloguing in Publication Data

Stromberg-Stein, Susan
Louis Dudek

Based on the author's thesis (M.A.--McGill University, 1977) entitled "A biographical introduction to Louis Dudek's poetry". ISBN 0-919614-50-7

1. Dudek, Louis, 1918- 2. Poets, Canadian (English) --20th century--Biography.* I. Title.

PS8507.U43Z875 1983   C811'.54   C84-090005-8   Pr9199.3.D83Z78 1983

Susan Stromberg~Stein

Louis Dudek
A Biographical Introduction to his Poetry

CHAMPLAIN COLLEGE
Golden Dog Press, Ottawa, Canada

Table of Contents

BIBLIOGRAPHY

List of Abbreviations

A.   *Atlantis* (1967)

C.   *Cerberus* (1952)

CP.   *Collected Poetry* (1971)

Dk.   *Dk/Some Letters of Ezra Pound* (1974)

E.   *Europe* (1954)

EC.   *East of the City* (1946)

Ep.   *Epigrams* (1975)

LS.   *Laughing Stalks* (1958)

M.   *En Mexico* (1958)

RC,   Recorded Conversations. Note: See Bibliography, p. 141

SI.   *The Searching Image* (1952)

TS.   *The Transparent Sea* (1956)

24P. *Twenty-Four Poems* (1952)

Prefatory Note

Biography can be one of the investigative tools employed to understand the process of creation. It was this possibility that prompted the study of the poet Louis Dudek, particularly because being present he is able to validate the facts of his life, and by revealing the biographical connections he can show us how the act of writing moves from fact to literary artefact.

When life becomes the subject matter for poetry, it is usually because it has been transformed to another level of meaning, a more universal one. A biographical study of this nature will reverse the creative process, so that certain details can be returned to their original state, to uncover pertinent elements about the life of the poet and to show the relation between these and the work itself.

What follows therefore is not a biography in the usual sense of the word. It is a biographical study to discover where and how the poetry intersects the poet's life. That is, whatever in the poetry is biographical is extracted, and that detail, which had been translated to the level of poetry, is then interpreted so that the same piece can be fitted into a jigsaw puzzle that will finally give us the portrait of Louis Dudek as man and artist. What is not present in the poetry, and is not essential to the complete story of the artist, has not been explored here to any great degree.

As the book evolves, the poetry gradually speaks to the reader more directly, as it should; so that, by the end, the creative life has become the poetry, achieving the final union between biography and literature – a life transformed into universal literary experience.

Writers prominent in Canadian literature who know Louis Dudek and who have been associated with him during the various stages of his career were interviewed in order to provide a further glimpse, both personal and critical, beyond the poetry, so that an alternative perspective of the man is also present in the text.

Susan Stromberg-Stein

Acknowledgments

To Social Sciences and Humanities Research Council of Canada for a research grant.

To Louis Dudek
for his time so generously given; for allowing me to scrutinize his poetry, and his life; for lending an able editorial hand.

To Desmond Cole
for his patient and generous assistance with the early drafts of this work.

To Mike Gnarowski
for his belief in the validity of this material and for seeing it through to publication.

To David Stein, Ilana and Marnie, Rhoda and the late Dr. Oscar Stromberg, Miriam Fletcher, Dr. Rachael Wasserman, Dr. Michael Brien – who have been motivating influences in my life.

To Lilian Dudek, Leonard Cohen, Ron Everson, Ralph Gustafson, D.G. Jones, Ken Norris, Frank Scott, Raymond Souster, Ronald Sutherland for their kind co-operation.

To Val Deker and Leena Corbett for patiently, and quickly, translating my illegible hieroglyphics into pages of neat black and white typescript.

"You've got to create something if you want it to exist."

– Louis Dudek

Chapter I

Introduction

In a paper presented at the Grove Symposium in 1974, Louis Dudek said: "At the core of every work of literature stands the self, or the psyche of the author; it is the first and most readily available ground for interpretation, the meaning from which all universal meanings spring, ..."[1]

The problem then is how much of the personal should be revealed, or can be revealed without invading the privacy of the poet or reducing the validity of the poetry as an artistic work. One of Dudek's *Epigrams* reads: "Fame is mainly the privilege of being pestered by strangers,"[2/] so that the main question that occurs regarding a study of this nature is whether, once the poet has published his work for the public, the reader has the right to pry beyond the written material. One fact is certain; the public will speculate about the poet and his life, so why not present the truth revealed by Dudek now while he is alive, in preference to vague theorizing about him after he is dead?

One cannot possibly transpose onto paper the mixture of feelings the poet experienced as he went through his work, poem by

---

* References to Louis Dudek's work will be indicated by abbreviation and page number following the quotation. See List of Abbreviations. Wherever possible *Collected Poetry* will be used.

1

poem, to search out the biographical element. The most curious aspect that surfaced as he re-read his early work was a bifurcation in that he would sit back after we finished a book and say with wonder, "That was someone I once was ... a man I used to know long ago." That man can view his life flowing before him from this perspective, witnessing the past in the present, is an unusual phenomenon that is often as painful as it is pleasurable.

The development that has taken place in literature of the twentieth century shows an increasing tendency towards revelation of the self; a greater number of biographical and autobiographical works have been published in this century than ever before. When Jean-Jacques Rousseau wrote *The Confessions* in 1770, he indicated in his first paragraph the singularity of his undertaking: "I have resolved on an enterprise which has no precedent, and which, once complete, will have no imitator. My purpose is to display to my kind a portrait in every way true to nature, and the man I shall portray will be myself."[3]

Interest in the individual self of the artist has become characteristic of twentieth-century literature and Dudek cites Rousseau as the initiator of this trend. "Rousseau is unique in that he turned his attention, and the attention of his readers, to his own personality, as no other writer had ever done before."[4]

Dudek adds that "Rousseau is the first writer in history for whom the facts of his own biography and the details of his personal feelings and experience are important in the interpretation of his work. He put the first person at the centre of things."[5]

In this spirit, then, let us examine the biographical facts relevant to the poet, Louis Dudek.

Chapter II

Family Background, Birth of Poet, Early Education

Louis Dudek was born on February 6, 1918 in Montreal, the middle child and only son of Vincent Dudek and Stanislawa Rozynska Dudek. He has one older sister, Lilian, and one younger sister, Irene, in his immediate family.

The father, Vincent Dudek, was born of Polish parents in 1891 in the Crimean area of Russia. The Russian government had forbidden the people to read, write or speak any language other than Russian. However, secretly by candlelight in the evenings, Vincent's grandfather taught the young boy to read and write Polish. In 1905, when he was fourteen, to avoid compulsory service in the Russian army, Vincent left his home and his family and, with the assistance of an uncle, successfully escaped to Canada and settled in Montreal.

Stanislawa ("Stasia") Rozynska was born in Liverpool, in 1895, the second of seven children. Being of Polish descent she grew up speaking both English and Polish. Her parents had fled from an area in Russia which is today Poland for the same reason that Vincent had fled to Canada. Survival was difficult for this family in Liverpool, and so her father, a carpenter by trade, decided to relocate his family in Africa. However, a ticket agent suggested that they would have the opportunity for a better life if they went instead to Canada. As a result, in 1902 they landed in Quebec. Stasia's mother was an energetic and capable businesswoman. She opened a grocery store in Montreal that sold everything from food to used furniture. This woman is remembered by her grandchildren as a loving matriarch.[6] Business improved and the Rozynski family gradually purchased the property they inhabited on Bercy Street, in Montreal's east end. In time they saved enough money to buy a farm at Charlemagne, Quebec.

The poet's mother was an artistic person. She sang beautifully, played the piano well, and read extensively. Vincent Dudek met Stasia Rozynska in the Montreal Polish community and they were married in June, 1915. The young couple settled at 2360 Bercy Street, next door to the bride's parents.

Vincent held several jobs after his arrival in Montreal. For a short time he taught Polish for the Montreal Catholic School Commission. As an immigrant he spoke little English and no French. At the time of his marriage he was a fireman for the St. Henri district. When Lilian was born he changed jobs and worked as a tailor for a clothing manufacturer. Louis was born in 1918. In 1920 Irene was born, and Vincent again changed jobs, this time to drive a delivery truck for the Frontenac Brewery.[7]

Louis Dudek grew up in a bilingual atmosphere — Polish and English. From the age of two he learned both languages at home. He recalls speaking Polish with the older people and English with his peers. His true mother tongue, as a result, is ambiguously referred to many years later in *Atlantis*:

> Jak to przyjemnie swój własny język usłyszyć!
>
> My true tongue.
> No, only another language,
> of childhood. (*A*.71)

The Polish line above means "How pleasant to hear one's own native tongue." We note the ambivalence: first the assertion, then the denial. Dudek now says that his true tongue is "Reality", not any particular language.[8] In high school, he added a working knowledge of Latin in addition to his reading and writing knowledge of English, French and Polish. Since then, through travel and study, he has become familiar with Greek, Spanish and Italian (*RC*, Feb. 10/77).

Very little of the poet's early childhood experience appears in his poetry. He refers to himself as "an immigrant's son" (*A*.113) in *Atlantis*, written at the age of forty-three. That so many years should pass and so much poetry be written before this mention of his ethnic origin brings to mind a passage from "The Prelude" by Wordsworth where the past life of the poet creeps innocuously into the present. In *Atlantis*, Dudek recalls "something you remember from way back to the beginning of life — a very early experience" (*RC*, Dec. 10/75).

> Dreams! ... Think of the real ghosts we knew!
> Something in the oval of that face
> surves her dream. (A.69)

The face in the above quotation has become an eidolon in the poet's mind. Such an eidolon would be the image of his mother who died on March 8, 1926, when he was eight years old. The boy was thus confronted with death, loss, and loneliness at an early age. According to his sister Lilian, the poet was the mother's favourite child, and as she lay dying her last thoughts were of him. Lilian describes her brother as having been a gentle, quiet child, unlike the other boys of his age in the neighbourhood.

There seemed to be a special affinity between Dudek and his mother. She particularly enjoyed spending her free time singing songs to him and telling him stories[9]. In 1951 he wrote a brief autobiographical sketch for Ryerson Press. In this sketch we find the only direct published statement about his mother. He describes her as: "an omnivorous reader, having gone through the English Bible, a manifest reading record."[10]

However, Dudek wrote one poem, in his middle life, about his mother: "The Loaded Gun" (unpublished):[11]

5

All I know is that they called her "Sis,"
the girl who was my mother.
I wonder what she was like. They said
she was the only one they knew
who'd read the Bible through
and I was her boy.
She must have had a head full of dreams...
Once, as a girl
she enacted a suicide before a mirror
with a real gun, pointing it at her head,
then fired at herself, pointing the gun at the mirror,
and the mirror crashed, the gun was loaded!
She fell in a real swoon. Lucky
to be like that. How was she, after?
She was young when she died. But not before she
    shaped me
just enough to make me as I am. I know. I might as well
look at myself. I dream too much, read too much.
And think of that gun sometimes, pointing.
It was loaded!...

There is a delicate interplay established in this poem between
past and present, between mother and son. Just as his mother read
extensively and was a dreamer, so the poet realizes that he has
these same tendencies. Even though their destiny is different, as an
extension of his mother "she shaped me/just enough to make me
as I am" the poet continues to "dream too much, read too
much." These characteristics denote the temperament of an artist
romantically conceived, a quality shared by both mother and son.

The same sense of loss and of longing for protection and
security is implicit in two romantic poems that were published in
East of the City, 1946, where nature becomes a metaphor to repre-
sent the poet's emotions. He remembers actually feeling a close
personal bond with nature (*RC*, Oct. 8/75).

Listen, how the rain mutters.
It is only a baby thing, being born
out of her mother cloud.

No harm to me. But I am smaller than this small rain:
it somehow surrounds me, and mothers me with its
   rainy arms. ("Shower," *EC*.6)

and in "Tree" he writes,

...my noblest tree.
Matronly, maternal, strong
green arm, and proud –

you hold the sky in your branches

I am in your shadow, tree. ("Tree," *EC*.7)

His expression of the child-parent relationship is specifically a longing for the mother-child relationship in these poems. Loss has created a romantic need for, and an openness to, the natural elements. There is perhaps a mental substitution, a personal literary personification, in this standard equation of nature as mother.

In retrospect, Dudek remembers he did not have as close a relationship with his father as he did with his mother. In the poetry he writes "In fact, we were always a bit distant." (*A*.93). His father was a rationalist with puritanical overtones and he firmly held to a code of right and wrong for his children. Louis recalls an incident that occurred near Bercy Street when he was a young boy. A soft drink truck had crashed and cases of soft drink were scattered over the street. The kids brought home some bottles, but they were severely reprimanded by their father and commanded to return them immediately to the scene of the accident (*RC*, Feb. 17/75).

The father directed his children's education. Louis' formal education began at five years of age when he attended Polish classes on Saturday mornings at St. Anselme School. He entered Lansdowne Elementary School the following year. Even though the Dudek family were Roman Catholic, Vincent managed to have his children admitted to the Protestant school system because he felt that too much of the curriculum in the Catholic schools was taken up with religious instruction. To qualify, the poet attended Protestant Sunday School, rather absurdly since the family also attended mass at the Roman Catholic Church. Later he said he

7

lived in some fear that he and his sisters might be removed from school. Today Dudek acknowledges that this double allegiance has perhaps resulted in a mind that is Protestant when he thinks and Roman Catholic when he feels. (*RC*, Nov. 11/76).

The father, after his wife's death, sent for his sister Walerya to come from Poland to help raise the three children. This aunt is remembered by the poet as a dear, self-sacrificing and devoted person. She was already forty years old when she came to Canada, and she never learned to speak English. A very shy person, she once told the boy about a single, memorable experience of her girlhood. This is recorded in the poem "Old Maid," a poem about his unmarried aunt:

> They ran barefoot over the sands,
> stringing their shoes around their necks.
> The sands were warm under the sun
> to the touch of the feet.
> The boys and girls
> ran on Sundays, home from the church...
> but I was always afraid.
>
> I was sixteen then;
> the boys would laugh
> at my white and delicate
> feet.
>
> And yet, sometimes,
> I dared
> to take off my shoes and run
> over the sands, home from church.
> Oh, the sun made the sands warm
> to the touch of feet! (*EC*. 13)

The title underlines her lack of self-fulfillment in marriage. It is clear the family she cared for did not fill the gap in her life, and in spite of her devotion, she could not fill the gap in theirs. After the mother's death, the children never mentioned the word mother at home. Sister Lilian says that when the three get together, even today, they talk about their father but only rarely and briefly about their mother[12].

When Dudek was not at school his favourite pastime was reading: "Books, however, were scarce in our home ... My childhood, apart from snow and rock fights with French Canadians and membership in the local gang of boys, was filled with reading novels of adventure, dozens of books from the local lending library and from a box of books stored in a back closet — translations of Edgar Rice Burroughs, also Sienkiewicz (*With Fire and Sword* and *Quo Vadis* among them). I later read Henty books and other boys' fiction; historical novels had the greatest appeal for me." [13] ...

It is interesting to note how, at this early age, the romance of history fascinated him, for this interest in history will recur later in his graduate studies.

Dudek's first poetic effort came when he was still in elementary school. "At about the age of eight or nine I wrote some verses about a cat and mouse which were thought to be surprising for my time of life ... while housework was going on, I began to extemporize comic-satiric squibs about members of the family ... The family was shocked at this discovery of talent." [14]

His aunt was literary, however, and well-read in Polish poetry, which she recited easily from memory. In the Ryerson biographical note Dudek remembers that she "read and recited some quantity of Polish romantic poetry ... notably Mickiewicz and Slowacki ... Slowacki, who appeared then as a kind of Polish Keats, made the strongest impression on me. My aunt was an excellent story-teller, ..." [15] The poet recalls, however, that the poetry that was on the public school curriculum "did not seem to leave any impression" on him. [16]

Perhaps this early lack is responsible for his involvement with the Canadian Council of Teachers of English, founded in Vancouver in 1967 and the delightful children's book he edited in 1973: *all kinds of everything*, which contains a variety of poems calculated to appeal to every child's imagination. Dudek's introduction to this book reflects his statement in *Atlantis:* "As for the little ones, teach them how to be happy — / it's their religion." (*A.93*) In the introduction he writes, "The world of play is a magic world — and strangely absorbing. Poetry is like that too. Poetry is a form of play ... We can think of poetry as a kind of spontaneous

9

happy life of the mind. It's the natural creativity of every living human being."[17]

It is evident that the absence of this type of book did not inhibit the poet's childhood interest in reading or writing verse. "In public school I remember showing the principal of the school a poem I had written and receiving his sympathetic comments."[18]

Moreover, an experience he carried into his adult life from elementary school is found in his poetry. Just as class was finishing for the day he glimpsed an airplane through the schoolroom window, a rare sight in those days, and he cried out with excitement. The teacher kept him in after class for this misdemeanour.

> I can remember
> walking down the corridor, later,
>   through the empty playground,
> looking up at the sky. There was nothing. (*A*.91)

The airplane here is a metaphor that describes the ephemeral quality of spontaneous joy and the experience of loss, as a general symbol for a wider loss.

Happiness and unhappiness are component emotions contained in the labyrinth of Dudek's memories of childhood for "childhood itself is only a copy/of some unimagined joy — /most of it tears, at imperfection." (*A*.92)

In the poems "Christmas" (*SI*.3) and "Romantic Lyric" (*CP*.13) written when he was in his twenties, the poet recalls two bleak and unhappy episodes from his childhood. The season in both poems is winter, and in both the poet is cold and unhappy. In the former he casts his thoughts back in time to Bercy Street.

> Recalling a green childhood choked with thistles,
> A patch of grassland sowed with crippling clinkers,
> Now walking in the park over ice-cream snow
> I am pierced by nails suddenly from frozen roots.
>   ("Christmas," *SI*.3)

In the bitter stanzas of this poem, the poet is "pierced by nails." Dudek thinks of this poem now as "leaden stanzas" written in "stress rhythm" (*RC*/74). Hyperbole emphatically conveys the poet's negative tone and attitude.

His association to cold is related to a painful childhood experience. As an infant his father left him outside in a sleigh while he went into a billiard parlour to talk with friends. The child nearly froze to death, and his health later was so poor that the family considered withdrawing him permanently from school. (*RC*, Nov. 26/74). So that when Dudek writes a poem about cold there may be a dimension of buried memory — or a sensitivity to cold — that goes very far back.

"Romantic Lyric" is a poem about childhood memories of wash day at home in east-end Montreal. The poem contains a reference to repeated illness, "waiting thin before the window" (*CP*.13), for he did not regain his health until he entered high school (*RC*, Nov. 24/74). The mood again is one of sadness for something lost.

> The cloth-white ferns on these winter windows
> remind one of Monday mornings, and frozen washing
> and billows of bubbling steam
> which would be rising from doorways.
>   I remember it all,
> as I stand at this window and watch the wind blow.
>
> O, but the weather's changed! I see the wind more
> than the ferns, and I am more cold than I was then.
> I do not love the warmth indoors either;
> no more, waiting thin before the window...
>   "Romantic Lyric," *CP*.13)

The "thin" young boy who froze in the sleigh experiences a more biting cold that cannot be removed by being in a warm house because it is an emotional chill. Now, the past remembered in "Christmas" is a warm coldness in contrast to the cold, however warm, present he experiences in "Romantic Lyric."

Dudek also records happy times from his childhood — for example, when he was ten years old there was his best friend, a boy named Peter, he says, "with whom I shared everything" (*A*.92) ...

> And a girl, aged eleven
> with long golden hair.

11

On the skating rink you took her hand
and went round and round. (*A*.92)

Looking back at his childhood, he finds that only then can one
find perfect trust (*RC*, Dec. 9/76) so that –

Some of the things we lose are better than what we find.
And we think the best must be copies of the life of a
child. (*A*.92)

He sees himself looking out of his bedroom window on Bercy
Street:

... remember summer
and golden sunsets
over back yards

Cats, clatter, and the tin horns
of yesterday
("Fragments 2", *CP*.297).

The discordant elements of happiness and unhappiness in his
life, and in his poetry, are best summed up in the following reflec-
tion: "I used to say that my childhood and my youth were the
most miserable time you can possibly imagine. I recovered a little
bit from it in my twenties and it turned into misery and suffering.
So there you are. One might say: Draw a curve of how good or bad
your life seemed to be – there are only *moments* that are good"
(*RC*, Nov. 13/75).

In 1931 he entered Grade eight at the High School of Mon-
treal. That he was a top student in Grade school is evident from
the fact that he missed winning a four-year scholarship by a few
marks – it went to a classmate named Harold Dickson. Neverthe-
less, the money was found for the high school fees. The school was
approximately two miles from his home, so he went by streetcar in
the morning, and to save the fare walked home in the afternoon
with a French companion, Guy Royer, who was also in the
English-Protestant high school.

Having spent more time nourishing his mind and imagination
than in playing with the children in the neighbourhood, Dudek
now became a high school student more interested in intellectual

12

pursuits than in athletic activities. By this time his sisters, who were active and practical, considered him the bookworm of the family. His sister Lilian recalls that she assumed Louis had inherited his mother's artistic qualities. [19] Dudek himself remembers that "... in high school I received some more stimulus to vanity ... Before the Christmas holiday one year the class teacher showed us a fountain pen and said it would go as a prize to whoever could write the best string of verses in five minutes. Everybody started scribbling. Then each pupil read out his effort. Some had three lines, some one, some a few words; a few had a completed verse. But near the end of the list I got up and in a nervous voice read out four quatrains, sixteen lines – a complete poem about Santa coming down the chimney. I won the pen by acclamation." [20]

Dudek won another poetry contest in his teens. "My elder sister ... also wrote verses. In about my fourteenth year we had a competition in poetry, with our parish priest (Father Bernard, a close friend) presiding as sole judge. A dozen lyrics by each were submitted, unsigned, all in the same handwriting: the judge was to divide them into two groups, or to give them a rating. The result was devastating to my sister, more triumphant for me than I wanted. All my poems were placed in the higher category." [21]

This positive reinforcement of his ability to write poetry perhaps had something to do with the poet's bravado in the following incident (*RC*, Dec. 10/76): "I was very fond of our Latin teacher in the last year of high school. To her I showed some bad versified translations of Horace and Catullus and communicated my desire to write poetry. I have never since been so entirely devoted to a poetic calling or career as then, nor so innocent in professing it." [22] Dudek chuckles as he reads the above passage today. "What an ass I was," he adds in the margin of the original manuscript.

By now he was thoroughly taken with the poetry on the high school curriculum: "poetry as a sort of musical language began to haunt me, and I carried around ... phrases of Byron, Keats, Shelley and Scott." [23]

Dudek spent his summer vacations at the Rozynski farm in Charlemagne, Quebec. It was during holidays spent there in the company of his cousins Alex, Adam and others, along with Father

13

Bernard, that some memorable incidents occurred to be referred to
years later in his poetry.

I had a recovery from a great headache one evening,
    it was in the country,
the sky a pale blue, and the air cool and fragrant.
The whole world was suddenly renewed. (*A*.91)

Then a dog was killed on the highway
and a boy wanted to take a gun
    and go out, and commit murder.

And two farming men
    faced each other with upraised pitchforks
in a quarrel over some cows.

And there was a priest who handed out candy. (*A*.92)

Happiness and misery are juxtaposed in this passage, as often
happens in his early poetry. The relief from a terrible headache ac-
centuates the peaceful serenity of a beautiful summer evening.
Death and discord shatter the calm, and there is the feeling of
shock and dismay as the world of experience penetrates the in-
nocence of the growing boy.

Still a devout Roman Catholic at the time, his innocent accep-
tance of church doctrines is undermined; the helplessness of the
"priest," Father Bernard, is apparent. This early memory marks
the beginning of Dudek's quest for personal truth.

The poet witnessed two fires when he was young. In Mon-
treal, at the age of fifteen, he watched a great church burn. The se-
cond fire occurred in the village of Charlemagne, close to the fami-
ly farm, when a butcher shop and adjacent buildings burned
down. He assisted at this fire by swinging buckets in a bucket
brigade to the burning buildings. What struck him was that he was
as helpless to put out these fires as the priest was to preserve the
old faith in the modern world.

I grew up, into some kind of manhood.
Ladling out water at a bucket-brigade at a great fire,
one day, seeing a church burn,
I saw how little can be saved. (*A*.92)

14

Unquestioning belief, we read, is reduced to ashes just as the church had been, and the poet realizes "how little can be saved." (*A*.92) He subsequently widened his reading to include the areas of history, philosophy and science, searching for the Lapis Lazuli, the hard truth to compensate for and replace the religious belief that had been lost. "It is not all that personal. Rather, it is a predicament of contemporary thought that I am concerned with," he comments in 1982.

"Until the age of about seventeen I had been a good Catholic, receiving Confession and Communion regularly once a month. In my late teens I went through a period of intense religiosity, and soon after broke with the faith completely. I was conscious of the incompatibility between natural sexual demands and the religious conception of sin; practical reason and scientific theory (evolution, geology, natural law) became my battering rams against religion. Nietzsche, D. H. Lawrence, Ibsen and Walt Whitman had their apotheosis; I considered myself an atheist and an anarchist."[24]

A poem from *Laughing Stalks* (1958), "The Changing World", shows Dudek's facetious attitude toward the authoritarianism of the church on matters of sex:

When the last Pope is dead, and the Vatican crypts are open
there will be —
after
2000 years
of
obfuscation,
inquisition,
forging of documents,
burning,
miseducation,
threats,
persecution
and
prohibition —

A Girl for every boy, and a Boy for every girl
(guaranteed by the State). (*CP*.186)

15

However, the poet apparently foresees that religious rule might be followed by authoritarian state control.

We see, then, that after high school he was already preoccupied with a personal quest and an intellectual dilemma which has engaged the modern world for centuries, and this philosophical concern has dominated his poetry from the beginning.

"I began to look ... seeking for what there is in actuality and in our brief lives, what there is in the actual that is not mere nothingness and emptiness ... the reality that is buried under reality ... I'm trying to understand what it is that has value and meaning, to rebuild the other half of possible existence."[25] The poet will come to the realization that,

> If we do not have religion, we must at least have
> philosophy.
> Or the unexamined life will become unlivable. (*A*.93)

The idea presented here is further explained by a theory of Dudek's about the historical function of philosophy: "Philosophy is an analysis, essentially of the religious problems, an attempt to retrench and to bolster up the declining religious order, to form a reconciliation between the old and the new − an effort in which the new inevitably triumphs."[26]

The poet throws light on his religio-philosophical position in a recent interview: "I'm not an anti-Catholic. I'm a lapsed Catholic. Be a believer in what you know. Life is a myriad-sided existence. Believe in it." (*RC*, Oct. 16/75).

Evil, however, is one component of this myriad-sided existence. Dudek will come to realize that Evil is as integral to mankind as Good.

> Evil is in the warp and weft of reality,
> but the whole cloth is good, is good.
> (*En Mexico, CP*.211)

A strong affirmation of life itself will become a predominant characteristic of the poet's sensibility. "... Look at the picture of La Primavera and think where that ecstasy came from in a world

16

of diabolical evil. There is something here; but what that is or what its ultimate meaning might be, has never been revealed to us. The answer is that it cannot be made clear — it's simply not possible. We know by knowing beauty and by responding to 'the light'. We know good and evil. At moments, something flows through us. 'God' is a constantly evolving possibility. There's no limit to experience. There's no finite resolution of all existence." (*RC*, Oct. 16/75).

The development outlined here did not, of course, come quickly or easily. What is central, and what began in his early teens, is the persistent attempt to resolve this profound uncertainty about the meaning of life.

It is also important to note that Canada at this time was in the throes of the great economic Depression of the 1930's[27]. In spite of the hardships Dudek's family suffered, money was found to enable him to go to college. He entered McGill in 1936 at the second year level, having completed grade twelve senior matriculation at the High School of Montreal, thus saving the cost of a McGill freshman year. His father remarried at this time and provided modest support during these difficult years. In the next chapter we will look at the poet's development against the social environment of the time, and we will follow his poetry through the period of the late thirties and forties.

Chapter III

Undergraduate Years,
Early Literary Life, and Marriage

Soon after registering in the Bachelor of Arts program at McGill University in Montreal, September, 1936, Dudek became a reporter for the *McGill Daily* and made his first appearance in print on October 6, 1936, the day of Fall Convocation.[28] Thereafter, he worked sporadically as a reporter until March 18, 1938 when he became one of seventeen associate editors,[29] a position he held until he completed his fourth year studies in May 1939. The final issue of the *Daily* for that year was printed on May 25, 1939, the day King George VI and Queen Elizabeth visited the McGill campus.[30]

In the Ryerson autobiographical sketch Dudek wrote: "I published items (as a reporter), some short articles, ... in the college paper, the McGill Daily ... I was only an average student in college; my idea of it, which still persists, was that it was a land of intellectual and social milk and honey ... Examinations seemed ridiculously easy, I passed them without any apparent work ... My practical objective at that time seemed to be newspaper work or journalism of some kind. Philosophy absorbed me, and I wrote dozens of dialogues in the Platonic manner, opposing the irreconcilable ideas that I had found in books."[31]

Dudek's fascination with "irreconcilable ideas" will result in an epigrammatic quality in his poetry that becomes apparent from *En Mexico*, 1958, and culminates in *Epigrams*, 1975.

Two youthful philosophical essays entitled "Life" appeared in the *McGill Daily* in 1937. One notes at once the vastness of his subject and the serious way he handles the material. The student of nineteen set out "... to show ... that there is a definite reason why intuitive knowledge must be true, and matter must exist ... And if we determine that argument ... is the road toward truth, then we shall be on the right path to the explanation of Life itself."[32]

Also, most interesting for the development of Dudek as poet is his concern in this early essay with the idea of "the image," a topic that is to haunt him throughout his career.

"Feelings, beliefs and emotions differ greatly from images which are called objects. What these images mean seems to be instinctively explained, for we never doubt that they represent substances external from the mind, but beyond instinct, in logic, their very nature will explain this ... images ... arc controlled by causes external to the mind ... This is because the causes lie in the things themselves."[33]

The ratiocination in these essays reveals a will to apply his mind, intuitive and practical, to the ambitious search for universal truth, a unifying set of relationships, and this is a quest that began, as we know, in-his late teens.

While taking courses at McGill, Dudek attended meetings of both the McGill Philosophy Club and the McGill Literature Society. At the former he met Stephanie Zuperko, a student of Lithuanian descent, who was to play an important part in his life; and at the Literature Society, he would meet, after graduation, an aspiring young poet, Irving Layton, who was to have a significant role in his early literary activities.

In the spring of 1939, Dudek graduated from McGill. The experience gained on the college paper was useful in his first job "doing odd paragraphs for the *Montrealer*."[34] This was only a part-time job, so he tutored a student from Three Rivers for some supplemental exams and soon after began free-lance work for an advertising agency. No regular work in journalism was available. Eventually he became a permanent copywriter with the advertising agencies. "... I was in a position to make a successful career in business. But I didn't take the opportunity,... I couldn't shape my mind to it and I hated the slick style and the false front about the whole advertising racket, ..."[35]

While working, Dudek continued writing poetry, a private interest he has enjoyed since he was eight years old. "I spent a good deal of my time writing poetry during working hours; ... I began to write a kind of poetry which I considered entirely my own and private ... experimental free verse ... I am astonished to remember that I had not the least idea of publishing them ... They seemed entirely unlike the romantic metrical poetry of the poets I once had admired; they were transcriptions of reality and of real feeling, often the most "unpoetical" things, and I hardly knew myself, though I felt it, that for the first time I was writing true poetry as it is always written."[36]

Finally, in the year 1941-42 eleven of his poems were printed in the *McGill Daily*, and the *Quebec Chronicle Telegraph* published several more in 1942.

Some of these early poems later appeared in *East of the City*. "Noon," "Skyscraper Window" (*CP*.17,18) and "Be Young With Me" (*EC*.40) give the reader a distinct impression of the poet's reaction to the working world. He hated office life and felt that he was caught up in the corruption of advertising.

> I had imagined that maggots had eaten me
> And abandoned my bones to the cheerless air,
> I had thought that death had made me a stone
> Dull to the sun, and to the life it sprinkles...
>
> ("Noon" *CP*.17)

During the noon break he would often leave the business section of Old Montreal and walk over to the students' union at McGill where he would have a snack and play chess. He also continued to attend meetings of the McGill Literature Society, and it was at one of these meetings in the fall of 1941 that he first met Irving Layton. They recognized each other's name because both had recently published poetry in the *McGill Daily*. On this common ground they became friends. Dudek remembers how, soon after they met, going for a walk over the Jacques Cartier Bridge, they discussed their future literary aspirations (*RC*, Mar. 15/77).

He wrote of this time in the autobiographical sketch: "By 1941 I had objectified this experimental verse somewhat ... About this time I met Irving Layton ... We quickly made friends and began to share enthusiasms both in poetry and politics; ... I had no head for political facts and theories, at least not at Layton's pace, ... For a time I supplied Layton with an example of his own conception of the true poetic personality, and I lived up to the idea."[37] One observes from the outset the individual differences between these two poets. Dudek's poetic stance, as we see to this day, is primarily philosophical rather than political.

Before long, Dudek and Layton's first wife Faye were preparing a dummy of Layton's first book *Here and Now* for the printer, a first editing job of this kind that Dudek was to do later for many poets. However, an event important to the future of both poets interrupted this undertaking. On one of his visits to McGill in 1942, Dudek met Professor Harold G. Files who taught a course in Creative Writing. (Dudek had not registered for this course but he remembers being very much aware of its existence.) The professor mentioned that he had seen Dudek's poetry in the *McGill Daily* and he recommended that Dudek get in touch with John Sutherland, who had just started the little magazine *First Statement*. At the beginning of December in 1942, Dudek and his new friend Layton met John Sutherland (*RC*, March 15/77). In a letter in 1974 to Michael Gnarowski, editor of *The Golden Dog*, Dudek refers specifically to the time and the issue in which he and Layton began their association with John Sutherland and the little magazine *First Statement*. "... this meeting must have occurred in December, or perhaps late in November 1942 ... Layton and I entered the picture with Vol. 1, No. 9."[38]

Dudek's association with *First Statement* marks the beginning of his literary career. He now had a steady outlet for the poetry he was writing, and he describes his work on the press: "... during the first year when the magazine was being printed I did much of the physical work on the press, because I was handy at it. Layton as a printer was more than useless (he in fact broke the press 'by getting

22

his head into it,' as I sometimes say − this is meant as a compliment − and the press had to be welded) ..."[39]

The poet finds delight in being smeared with the black ink from the printing press because from this dirtiness art must come. It is the other dirt of civilization, emanating from man's ignorance and vulgarity, that he is unwilling and unable to tolerate: (*RC*, Sept. 23/76)

> I gag at vulgarity
> − an immigrant's son, who like work and wash-up,
>   printing, against the dirt of creation,
> poems or books − (*A*.113)

Dudek became active on *First Statement* in the midst of what has been described as a "literary revival in Canada."[40] The country was just coming out of the Depression and was involved in World War II. "Under the stimulation of renewed prosperity and national excitement ..."[41] an increased amount of poetry was being written and new literary magazines and presses were established that furthered the beginning of the modernist movement. The new poetry had begun in the twenties with the Montreal Group − Scott, Klein, Kennedy and Smith − and now in the forties it expanded with the arrival of a new generation of poets. "Never before had there been so many interesting poets writing in Canada at one time."[42]

"... Dudek, Layton, Souster, and Waddington wrote their moving personal lyrics or their bitter commentaries upon a disordered civilization ... It was a period of ... impassioned debates about the nature and aims of poetry and in particular about its responsibility to society."[43]

Dudek's belief in the validity and importance of Canadian poetry led to his generous financial contributions to *First Statement*; also it marked the beginning of his financial aid to a series of small press books. While working for the Canadian Advertising Agency, part of his pay cheque and most of his spare time were invested in this little magazine.

In the summer of 1943 he wrote an article for *First Statement* entitled "Poets of Revolt ... or Reaction?" discussing the reexamination and redefinition of the purpose of poetry in Canada during this period. The new Canadian poetry he championed was to be in free verse rather than in the conventional stanza form employed by earlier poets. Carl Sandburg, Walt Whitman and Edgar Lee Masters are cited in this article as initiators of a new realistic style in poetry. As opposed to previous romantic authors, Dudek felt that the subject matter of poetry should be concerned with "the existing world of business, industry, radio, taxes, noise." His belief was that no contemporary poet "can escape from it: the noise of democracy has broken down all walls."[44]

"The poets of the past have been sheltered from real contact – at best they have idealized the people – and they have always managed to avoid them. Today, a revolution is being accomplished, in which all white shirts are soiled ... Poets are dragged into the streets ... Neither do the real poets of the people mind it ... This is one key to the enigma of the modern revolt in poetry."[45]

The editorial policy of *First Statement* magazine was to print literature "which will reflect the atmosphere and currents of Canadian life," as long as "re-acting honestly ... first hand" is the "chief concern of the poet."[46]

Dudek's poetry at this time reflects his conviction that "the real," however degraded, is the material from which poetry should come. The following uncollected poem "The People Like It" expresses his persistent theme that the mass media, serving special interests, exploit rather than serve the people.

The girl behind the 10¢ lunch counter
Said to me, confidentially:
"We feed them anything.
I've seen them after ten years.
It does them no harm."
The same thing was said by a man behind a radio station:
"We feed them crap.
Anything goes if they like it.
I sells. It does them no harm."
In the newspapers it's all the same.
Behind the flag-waving and the cheek-kissing
It's all the same.
It's the same in governments

Both of cities and nations.
And in the churches, too.
They feed you crap.
(Sometimes they are best-intentioned, they have
    nothing better to give.)
And you, the people,
Like it —
It does you no harm!

The poet's anger is directed not only at the church but at all facets of society that are in a position to control and influence whatever it is that the people are fed. Through his poetry he hopes to waken them from their indifference and lethargy and incite them to react against the injustices in society. In the same way he delivers a devastating condemnation in his poem "Be Young With Me" — "But carry an ax of stone to this murderous civilization." (*EC*.40).

Many imagist poems from this period are written from first-hand observation of the working world, for example: "Old City Sector," "Looking at Stenographers" (*CP*.7,38), "After Hours," "Basement Workers" (*EC*.22,34), "Building a Skyscraper," and "East of the City" (*CP*.44,33).

Critics of the early poetry have sometimes seen Dudek as a leftist, a Marxist, a Socialist, an anti-capitalist. However, in light of his particular background (his father, too, was a worker), the following lines can be understood without attaching any of the above political adjectives. Primarily the poet is a humanist.

We will praise "Men Working." They will be celebrated
more than millionaires, since without rich men
nations can run as well, or better, but not without these men.
    ("Building a Skyscraper" *CP*.45)

These lines reflect Dudek's feelings that the worker provides the material goods on which society is built. Here Dudek has corrected what he believes to be a misconception about our scale of values — the worker is to be exalted for his labour, not the rich man for the power and position that his money buys.

In March 1943, Dudek and Layton first met Raymond Souster, visiting from Toronto, at the *First Statement* office. The three young poets became good friends and their names were to be linked together from that time on; in fact, they often wrote poems on the same subjects. Dudek's "Paint" (*EC*.20) may have given Layton the idea to write "Westmount Doll."[48] Dudek wrote "The Diver" and Layton wrote "The Swimmer."[49] His early poem about the falls is "Midsummer Adirondacks" (*CP*.17) and Souster's, written some years later, "At Split Rock Falls,"[50] deal with the same locale.

"Midsummer Adirondacks" was written while Dudek was in what he calls the midsummer of his life. At the *First Statement* office in 1942 he met Stephanie Zuperko again, whom he had known from the McGill Philosophy Club. A friendship quickly developed. On a bicycle trip in the Adirondack region they stopped for a picnic at Split Rock Falls, south of Elizabethtown on the Bouquet River. The setting, imagery and symbolism depict the celebration of that love.

> There in the hills, we kissed.
> In the streams, pebble-naked
> – your body bread-brown, then shining,
>   shining with drops, bewildered with water –
> your kisses bright as those berries I had,
> kissed your lips like a rock, with mad water kisses.
> (*CP*.18)

Dudek describes the scene as a place where water "comes crashing down the crevasse while one stands above this great canyon" (*RC*, Mar. 25/75).

"A Young Tree" (*EC*.2) is a poem for Stephanie, as were many others at this time. Before this, the tree has been described in Dudek's poetry as "matronly, maternal, strong" ("Tree" *EC*.7). Now the tree, representing the young girl, is a "Sapling" that requires tender and gentle care.

> And daily now, in the garden grove,
> That young tree
> Grown tall in the tender, quiet air
> I guard and love. (*EC*.2)

26

In this poem, also, the prospect of marriage is suggested: "I think of an arbour for my bride" (*EC*.2). Now the poetry of trees contains a warmth which was not in his imagery before; a contrast to the earlier emotional chill perceived in "Romantic Lyric" and "Christmas" (p.8).

> Her voice comes to me
> not from the cold winter
> not from the distance
> but from within me. ("Her Voice ..." *EC*.8)

"Gift Poem, Bohemian" is a birthday poem written a few months later. Assuming the role of the troubadour, he writes to "Delight my love's heart!" (*EC*.15). The poem he writes is a more precious gift than any trinket he could buy.

On September 16, 1944 the couple were married at the St. Thomas More Roman Catholic Church in Montreal. A happy spirit pervades the love poems from this period. In these poems Nature itself often becomes a metaphor for the lover's emotions.

> Most men give flowers in their full leaves,
> But I give you flowers still in seed:
> These flowers you see are each one wrapped
> In the womb, still concentrated in sap.
>   ...
> So you and I, when these plant leaves appear
> Like days unfolding in the calendar,
> Will watch the flowers sent out in shoots
> And love grow out of its mysterious roots.
>   ("Flower Bulbs" *CP*.48)

Stephanie had also been working for a large advertising agency, however a few weeks after the wedding they both resigned from their copywriting jobs and set out to begin a new life together in New York City. "With my marriage ... I separated myself from the magazine (*First Statement*) and went with my wife to live in New York. We went to New York without any special purpose, except to get away from the advertising business ... and in order to see the great world. Soon, however, we became ... interested in the possibility of serious study at Columbia University; my wife began her graduate studies in psychology and I in history."[51]

Louis Dudek's life takes another turn at this point. Academic achievement, literary work, new friendships, and personal disappointment will mark the following eight years he will spend in New York.

Chapter IV

The New York Years

In New York the young couple found a one-room apartment near Columbia University on 123rd Street and Amsterdam Avenue. In a short time both enrolled in graduate programs at Columbia. They also found part-time employment. "Money was tight," Dudek remembers, "but the life of freedom was good" (*RC*, Oct. 16/75).

For a History M.A., Dudek began a study of the literary profession: "William Makepeace Thackeray and the Profession of Letters." The study of Thackeray, the great nineteenth-century satirist and realist, would expand later into a general concern with the social role of the artist. Dudek studied under the Canadian historian J. B. Brebner, in the M.A. course, and later in Comparative Literature, under Emery Neff, Lionel Trilling and Jacques Barzun. The poetry he was writing at this time touches on many aspects of his New York experience.

"A Store-House" deals with the intellectual isolation of the poet in the big city. The setting is a storage shed behind a laboratory at Columbia University, the lab where Dudek had a part-time job washing bottles and delivering dangerous chemicals to the scientists. World War II was raging and researchers were working on the control of malaria. Mike Gnarowski notes that

Dudek has a certificate signed by President Roosevelt acknowledging his contribution to the war effort.

In this poem the poet's imagination converts the storage shed to a symbolic hermit's cave where he can "sit, leaning and looking at the samplings I get/of the world" (*CP*.39). Just as these samplings are isolated in the shed, so, too, is the poet:

> But I know that no one will look into my door –
> the people pass by too busy. (*CP*.39)

In New York he feels himself cut off from his literary companions, and he records his solitude:

> Perhaps I will meet other men sitting in doorways,
>   sad as I am;
> if I find them, we will sit aside somewhere
> and talk this over. (*CP*.39)

The dilemma of the modern artist, observing life rather than participating, is evident here, and this becomes particularly significant if one recalls Dudek's theory in "Poets of Revolt ... or Reaction" that the new poetry should portray in a realistic manner the shape of everyday life. Dudek, however, is no longer employed and engaged as he was in Montreal, but sees himself cut off from life, in contemplative isolation.

"A Store-House" marks the poet's commitment to a life of intellectual pursuit that first began in Montreal. The didactic or prophetic direction Dudek's career will take in the near future is indicated:

> And sometimes I want to cry, and sometimes to call out,
> to raise a banner before my shack, make up a congregation.
>   (*CP*.39)

Clearly, the poet should be a prophet, a bringer of new knowledge to the world (*RC*, Apr. 16/75). This didactic purpose will influence his choice of career, and it will be evident in many different forms in his future writing.

The way Dudek views New York gives the reader some indication of his experience in that city. In the poem "Broadway" (*EC*.21), New York is seen as an unreal place – a circus in full swing. The poet stands back, alone in the crowd, and sees the scene in terms of these circus images. Amidst the commotion of dancing and swinging and laughter with bright flashes of colour, he suddenly cuts across the scene with horror to the tragic opera *I Pagliacci*, also about the circus. In the clown's face he sees the agony of Cannio and the tragedy of love and despair.

> ... but in spite of the noise
> the flowers of light and the laughter,
> you can see in the big clown's wizened face
> Columbine's pleading eyes and the dagger,
> and on a sudden, crazed Cannio's stagger. (*EC.*21)

Close examination of the New York poetry reveals a tragic element previously absent in the Montreal poems. In "Meditation Over a Wintry City" he writes about man in general –

> having eaten strange fruit he goes
> drunk with wild passions, in crooked ways,
> an enemy to strangers, unkind to his own kin. (*CP.*30-31)

And in "The Dead" he writes:

> 'I remember,' and here he bit his lip out of ancient habit,
> 'that even love was painful.' (*CP.*73)

Dudek's marriage broke up during the years in New York. The steps from early love to the marital break-up can almost be traced in the poetry.

"Come On, Mr. Freud" is a fictional dream poem. His wife was studying to be a clinical psychologist (under Dr. Zymunt Piotrowski) and part of her course requirement was to undergo therapy. The poet, engrossed in the study of history, pretends to parody Freudian psychological interpretation as he rattles through his dream.

> I dreamed that I was sitting with God on my knees
> While three unhappy hanged men whistled in the trees;
> A stream was flowing by of curdled blood and milk
> With a lady in the current wrapped in blood-stained silk.
> (*SI.*8)

The poet, however, still enjoys the erotic experience despite the grumbling protestations of God.

> The girl drowned in purple awoke from her dream,
> The milk turned to water, the blood to pebbles green;
> I kissed and held her, and laughed without a sound,
> While God, the great turtle, rumbled underground.
>
> (*SI*.9)

Today, the poet remembers this period as one of the less happy times of his life, but paradoxically he "wouldn't mind living it over again," because as he says, "experience is *the* thing, no matter whether it was painful or not" (*RC*, Apr. 8/75).

The poem "Quarrel" is an even more explicit projection of marital conflict:

> Bitch
> Beast Buffoon Egoist
>   Catface
>   You.
>
> Emerald eyes
> your forehead is white as a September morning
>   but I have grown tired of loving,
>
> even your beauty
>   can no longer move me,
>
> like an autumn leaf
> you wither in my eyes to ashen grace. (*CP*.71)

And yet we come in the last three lines to a reconciliation between the lovers:

> Why should we quarrel then?
>   Let us kiss
>   and put wisdom into each other's mouth. (*CP*.71)

"Golden Hands," another poem of this period, was apparently written during a separation. The meaning of this poem is somewhat ambiguous. One would presume that the speaker is deeply attached, from the line — "Death could not reach me in your ultra-violet arms." (*SI*.9) Yet on the other hand,

32

Backbirds have cawed you home since, and the snake
Chased you from perch to perch on the embittered lake (*SI.*9)

There is a transition to hideous images of distress in the last three stanzas. He realizes that once love has been broken it cannot be rebuilt, and it will take years before he will resolve this conflict in his personal life.

Just as one becomes aware of the personal dimensions of this poetry so it becomes evident that there has been a subtle change in the content of the New York poems. The outlook, instead of being localized as in the Montreal poems, is now more cosmopolitan or universal. Study at Columbia has broadened Dudek's knowledge and contributed to a wider poetic vision.

"A Hebrew Seminary" is a sample of the widened historical perspective in the New York poetry. The Seminary was near the university and Dudek passed it frequently. In the poem, it becomes a symbol of high intellectual and religious vision, of ageless truth, as perceived by the human spirit. Dudek finds in the Jewish religion an apocalyptic wisdom that he could not apply at this time to the Roman Catholic Church (*RC*, Apr. 15/75).

> The white wall of the Hebrew seminary in the moonlight
> is like the face of a Levite after long fasting and prayer;
> it has all the intellectual beauty of his race,
> and on the parchment of the face, are thin lines of
>   suffering.
>
> The white wall of the Seminary
> motionless as a veil in moonlight,
> is apocalyptic, old, yet without age;
>   but soon it will be erased, lost to mind,
> with the morning, when the sun crashes on the ghettos.
>   (*EC.*27)

Another example of this larger perspective occurs in "Appendectomy" (*CP.*52), a poem following surgery in a New York hospital. As the surgeon removes the diseased organ from the body, the poem tells us the ills of society need surgical treatment. Society, however, fails to seek a cure.

He looks from the evening window at the social body
Where appendices and cysts in bloom perpetually explode.

(*CP*.52)

There is a marked realistic, philosophical development in two New York poems: "The Great As If" and "The Dead" (CP.70,73) – poems in which the poet comes to terms with and defines his conception of death. The first ends with a question about life and human mortality.

What, then, was this life?
Where was this world –
when all will be as if it had not been? (*CP*.70)

The second poem, "The Dead," presents a view of life and death from the afterworld, as though answering the question posed in the first poem. Here the poet is comparing life to life-after-death.

'I'm glad, said one, looking back toward the earth.
I'm free of it, I'm no longer one of them. I am glad'.
... The worst of it was, as I see it now' ... (he
looked out across the plain into the grey distance
without obstacle) 'was to be caught in a net that did
not even exist.' (*CP*.73)

The poem concludes, as did Chaucer's Troilus,[52] with an affirmation of joyful existence after death, though the statement remains somewhat ambiguous.

... a dark cloud passed over us, and the
earth was blotted out.
... And then we were
bathed in a morning light of sudden gladness. And there
was nothing. (*CP*.73)

"Meditation Over a Wintry City" further explores a wider range of poetry. The tone and the content is philosophical in its depth and seriousness. Having touched on life and death, the poet contemplates the reality of existence:

To live. To breathe the crystal air
yet a while longer. To hold this shape and motion

34

and precarious mind unbroken ... .
... To hold anxiously
to the crumbling earth, and swim
still in the sea of air and light ... .
... there is a glorious logic and a god
in every force that moves a life ... . (*CP.*29)

In geological terms the life of man is but "A quiver in Space-Time" ("Relativity" *CP.*66),

but who would turn from it, the living of it,
on that account?
We hang on as long as we can
and hate to think how quick it flies.
("A Short Speech" *CP.*153)

The poet, also, has an important function in Society.

Stalked by disease and death, as all men are,
drowned in the apparent chaos of these times,
artists and scholars walk their quiet ways,
echo the pain that other men should feel, and understand,
and make their voices heard as something seen, above all sound.
("Meditation ..." (*CP.*32))

In larger terms, Dudek aspires in his life and his poetry to achieve the Greek notion of the cosmos: "the justice or harmony,"[53] in contrast to earthly chaos. So in the poem "Kosmos: The Greek World," this is the Greek achievement:

What memory of pain
he then denied, fought, shut his eyes to,
or reconciled,
to make that intellectual gain! But he did.
...he found everything to praise. (*CP.*130)

"Praise" is an adjective that will describe life in the later poetry. He has experienced tragic despair, deep philosophical questioning, and finally, he has reached a positive philosophical awareness of man's place in the cosmos during the eight years in New York.

35

An example of this new attitude to life is seen in the poem "Hot Time" (*CP*.62), written for Herbert Gold, the American novelist who lived near the poet in New York. Gold was writing his first novel when the two writers met and they played handball together on Morningside and 125th Street on a very hot day. The absence of isolation and rumination here is notable, and Dudek has said that "the sense of friendship, with no inhibitions" made this afternoon memorable. "I really believe in life, experiences of this kind, certainly not in ideas alone." (*RC*, Oct. 8/75).

There is another interesting friendship the poet made in New York; a lady described in the poem "To A Literary Patron" (*CP*.50). Dudek chuckles as he reads this poem thirty years later — the standard "Portrait of a Lady" in modern poetry: "I once drank coffee at your sun-stained window."

Playing the role of the tortured aesthetic poet, he sees himself as the poet-friend of 'a society lady', who invites the literati to her home overlooking the George Washington Bridge. She offers coffee, charm, and moral support. He gives her flattery in return, with a twinge of guilt at his own hypocrisy. The voice of the poet here is decidedly ironic. He was influenced by his reading at this time of analogous poems by T. S. Eliot, Ezra Pound, and by Henry James' novel *The Portrait of a Lady* (*RC*, Oct. 8/75).

During the eight years in New York, Dudek corresponded with his Montreal friends, and on occasion would visit them during vacations. His poetry continued to appear from time to time in *First Statement* and subsequently in *Northern Review*. In 1944 during the first year in New York, he saw his poetry published in book form. *Unit of Five* contained poems written by himself, Raymond Souster, P. K. Page, Ronald Hambleton, and James Wreford. Then *East of the City* was published by Ryerson Press in 1946, the year Dudek successfully completed his M.A. This book is the first separate collection of his poems. The form of his later verse will evolve from the free verse style employed in this book, most typical in the poem "On Poetry" (*CP*.24). Douglas Barbour describes Dudek's poetry during this period: "The poems about the city, usually New York, ... relate to the social-consciousness poetry of the thirties, but once again reveal the philosophical interest with which Dudek approaches all his subjects.''[54]

Dudek's growing interest in the sociology of literature is evident in his choice of a thesis topic. While working on his Master's degree in history he came to know J.B. Brebner, under whom he took a tutorial course for one semester. A.G. Bailey, poet and professor at Fredericton, New Brunswick, recommended Dudek to Brebner in a personal letter at the time. The following year Brebner invited Dudek, along with Emery Neff, for dinner at the Columbia. Thorndike's *Literature in a Changing Age* and Neff's *Carlyle* clearly provided the lead for Dudek's growing interest in the sociology of literature.'' [55]

"Neff was a scholar in the tradition of A. H. Thorndike at Columbia. Thorndike's "Literature in a Changing Age" and Neff's "Carlyle" clearly provided the lead for Dudek's growing interest in the sociology of literature.''[55]

Dudek's explanation of this development is found in his "Autobiographical Sketch." "I had now come to realize that literature was my proper field, and that my desire to understand economics and history was simply part of a desire to find a sound basis for understanding poetry and its history. As in my experiments with free verse in 1940, I had apparently gotten away from poetry only to come nearer to it.''[56]

This broadening of interests is evident in two poems written at Columbia. The poet who "grew up into some kind of manhood" (*A*.92) now sees a divine process operating in nature and in human history. "Flowers on Windows" and "Coming Suddenly to The Sea" reveal an emotional and philosophical development, and an excitement about new depths of meaning and significance, that mark a new stage of the poetry.

> Men move mountains and build their cities;
> and yet, the only answer one would like to find,
> the Fact the mind would embrace as a lover
> and would greedily uncover under the design —
> is the city built within him that moves a man!

> Though lost in the ignorant traffic, still I would rejoice.

> There is some hidden wisdom in all gardens,
> cities, in the leaves of flowers, the eyes of boys!
> ...
> All moves with a hidden meaning; only the fool
> denies God — even as the priest-fool simplifies.
> ...
> What is there in man which builds a city?
> And where the original city he began?
> I have ravaged the womb, and the planted seed,
> and moved mountains of knowledge for this gold.
> Now look upon the surface — how these flowers unfold!
>   ("Flowers ..." *CP*.46)

The cosmic and aesthetic principles have come together in this poetry.

In "Coming Suddenly to The Sea" the poet's twenty-eight-year "infant eyes" are suddenly opened as he contemplates a force infinitely stronger than man — the sea — symbolic of all creative nature. It will become a unifying leitmotif in his future poetry, though already in this poem it is the "mother of all things that breathe," the "Sower of Life," and also the antithesis — "terrible as a torch," as well as "carnivorous." The poet who came to the sea in all innocence leaves with a revelation of great importance for his future thinking.

> And so I brought home, as an emblem of that day
> ending my long blind years, a fistful of blood-red weed in
>   my hand. (*CP*.59)

The language of this poem is hard and concrete; never abstract. It is highly sexual, without being ethereal. The sun, the water, and the weed are all vibrant images. The poet is actively involved, speaking in the first person singular. He has lost his "infant eyes" for a deeper sight and vision. The sea, that has the power to batter "a granite rock to make it a pebble," (*CP*.59) has also the power to awaken in the mind a deeper cosmic awareness.

A further event at this time is Dudek's correspondence and eventual meeting with Ezra Pound. Before leaving Canada, he knew only Pound's early poems, the *Personae*. While living in

New York he read *The Cantos* and his interest in Pound grew rapidly. At this time World War II came to an end and Ezra Pound was brought back to the United States to stand trial for treason. Dudek saw in Pound a fine tenderness and humanity and he recognized in Pound primarily a dedication to the art of poetry. Out of sympathy he wrote Pound a friendly note in 1949. Hardly expecting an answer, he was surprised when a reply arrived on June 1, 1949. Their correspondence continued until September 4, 1967.

Ezra Pound first appears in Dudek's poetry in 1949 just after their correspondence began.

For E. P.

> For Christ's sake, you didn't invent sunlight;
> There was sun dazzle before you, and stricken leaves,
> *Phoibos* of the goddamned "narrow thighs" –
> But you talk as if you made light or discovered it. (*C*.28)

This poem expresses a tough ironic reaction to Pound. "Obviously I admire him immensely," Dudek says later about this poem, "but I resent him too – for being so magnificent" (*RC*, Dec. 9/76). The energetic outburst in these four lines is an unusual occurrence for the young poet. In his book *Dk/Some Letters of Ezra Pound* he explains the great love and admiration he had for Pound: "That I have loved Pound is perhaps apparent from all this scribbling. That I have loved him for the joy and the dazzling luminosity of his rich compacted poetry – his vocabulary of proper nouns alone is greater than any, and his monetary magic turns even lead to gold – was made clear in a poem ("For E.P.") I wrote for him way back in 1949." (*Dk*.145).

Over the years critics have accused Dudek of 'aping Pound'. Irving Layton claims that "meeting Pound was hard on Dudek because in trying to reach up to Pound's level he never developed his own poetic voice."[58] Any close interpretation and examination of Dudek's poetry, however, will show Layton's statement to be quite mistaken. The development and maturation of the early symbols and the imagery characteristic of Dudek's poetry, such as sun, flowers, and sea, are undisturbed and continuous; and his philosophical voice is continuous also from the early poetry to the most recent work. Quite peculiar to himself, Dudek developed a deeper understanding of the truth of existence, year by year, out of his continued observation, experience, and education. In line with this, his style developed, and remained his own, quite distinct from anything in Ezra Pound.

Pound personally arranged that Dudek meet and correspond with several literary people in the United States: thus association with Cid Corman, Paul Blackburn, Marianne Moore, William Carlos Williams, resulted in contacts and discussions important to Dudek's development as a poet and to his writing the new kind of poetry he felt was necessary. As well, when the Dudeks travelled to Europe for the first time in 1953, Pound gave Dudek a list of literary figures to call on. "I made efforts to reach all these people, but of the lot Christopher Logue, English poet then living in Paris, Peter Russell, the editor of *Nine*, and Jerzy Niemojowski became good friends. Logue introduced us to Alexander Trocchi and the group around Merlin, as well as to the writings of Samuel Beckett, ... Niemojowski brought us in contact with Czeslaw Bednarchyk and the Poets' and Painters' Press in London, which printed most of the Contact Press books for a number of years." (*Dk*.100).

Dudek's poem "The Pomegranate" appeared first in *Imagi* in 1950 opposite a poem by Marianne Moore. She wrote complimenting him and he recalls this with his wonderful humour: "We were between the sheets together − in this instance!" The names of these friends occasionally appear in Dudek's poetry, for example:

> There was a ship's lock on Russell's door,
> the literary place
> of England.
> We talked about Pound and bragged. (*E*.41)

Later in *Atlantis*, after the poet's second trip to Europe in 1961, Dudek recalls his meeting with another Pound contact, the English poet Michael Shayer. Their encounter appears in a passage of the poetry: "... go to Shayer's" (*A*.116). What is so interesting about this meeting is that neither poet had seen the other, yet they met on crowded Oxford Street in London as if they knew each other at sight. "We didn't describe ourselves, poets rarely need to" (*A*.118). The scene is recorded in the poetry exactly as it happened. The further information omitted is that Dudek spent a weekend in the north of England with Shayer and his wife Abba, (*A*.119) at their country house, following the London meeting. (*RC*, Sept. 23/76).

The exchange of ideas, the discussion of personal goals and literary aims with these people, precipitated by Pound, would last many years and contribute to expanding the poet's literary and intellectual horizons.

From time to time, Dudek sent Ezra Pound poems that he was translating from Greek and Latin, for Pound's opinion. There is usually a biographic aspect to the poems that Dudek chooses to translate; in fact, in almost every case the translation is an objective correlative for something the poet feels or wants to say. Examples of the poems Pound saw are "Phainetai Moi ...," "Alba" (*C*.27,29), "From Catullus" (*TS*.73) and "Pratinas Against the Flute" (*C*.29). All these poems were highly worked up. There were 130 drafts, for example, of "Pratinas Against the Flute" before Dudek was satisfied. Pound had recommended that Dudek omit the first four words in the last line of "From Catullus." Dudek disagreed, "Pound's corrections did not seem feasible." (*Dk*. 114).

On Dudek's first trip to Europe in 1953, he had stopped in Siena to visit Olga Rudge, Ezra Pound's one-time mistress (*E*.98). By the time he made his second trip, in 1961, Pound had been released from St. Elizabeth's hospital and was in Rome. Unfortunately he had suffered a stroke. As Dudek writes in Atlantis:

> I went to see one of the gods
> > still living
> Ezra Pound
>
> the greatest river god of them all
> dying, in a great bed, into immortality ... . (*A*.55)

He had brought Pound news of his son Omar, who had married a Montreal girl, Elizabeth Parkin.

> And he said...
> > well, nothing

>Only the tears filled his eyes
>as the great heart beat badly (*A.56*)

Dudek's grief at seeing this grand loquacious master unable to speak a word having suffered physical and mental anguish, is expressed with fine sensitivity. He feels helpless. Neither moral support nor friendly communication could help Pound in his suffering. "And I walked around that place a little, and went my way." (*A.56*)

During the years that Pound was imprisoned at St. Elizabeth's Hospital, in Washington D.C., he bore numerous blows to his human dignity. It was Dudek's opinion that "his narrow dogmatism was a product of his mental illness; but this illness, ... was a surface mania" (*Dk*.90). That Dudek had the compassion to somehow alleviate a small portion of this great man's suffering ("... devastating and tragic for him ...") (*Dk*.90) is a characteristic that both men had in common: tenderness and gentleness.[59] Neither would kill a spider (*Dk*.30), or an ant.

>The longer one lives
>the more tolerance one learns.

>To be kind and love
>green frogs, ghost crabs, snakes.
>All those gentle mechanical creatures
>that we kill.
>To save man from his insanities.

>(With tender affection
>I flick an ant to the ground:
>"Go along, now.") (*En Mexico*, *CP*.210)

The poet's profound respect for all forms of life appears throughout his writing. Being a realist, however, he notes that society's interpretation of love may often be superficial, or stand on a purely physical level: "you will find.../in the meeting of bodies,/we are still apart." (*A*.77)

>It's difficult to love. Maybe impossible.
>How can we 'love one another'?
>At best we can only pretend.

How to be able to love – anything, anyone!
– It's the main object of life, of art.

(*A*.119)

For this poet, the important quality in love is not physical passion, though we learn something important from it.

What would it all mean if it weren't for lovers,
the young, with love in their eyes?
And where would we get the language of paradise?

(A.78)

Compassion is an emotional quality necessary in love, that can bring the world together: "Love ... for the small dog, the hungry rabbit, the wild/mustang ... / or you cannot even love a woman." (*A*.112) Dudek notes that Arthur Miller was making a point about compassion in the "mustang" reference, in "The Misfits," while the critics, who are the real misfits in this case, assumed the film was about "the battle of the sexes" (A.112). Like Plato, Dudek believes in "loving earthly things" and he strives to emulate the Greek ideal as shown in their gods – "delicate, vulnerable-/their gentleness and gracefulness/a harmonious union of the elements" (*A*.123). Ezra Pound, according to Dudek, was a poet who worked close to the Greek ideal, despite his illness and his obsessions.

Meanwhile, Dudek continued his studies at Columbia University. In the same year that he entered the doctorate program in Comparative Literature he began teaching evening classes to undergraduates at the City College in New York City, "... the usual composition classes and literature surveys of the first and second years. I thought of myself now as a teacher with a useful status in society; I could believe in my work, a privilege which I felt that few occupations today can provide."[60]

His reaction was quite different from what he felt working in the advertising field. "I also began to see that this work (teaching) is not necessarily antithetical to the writing of poetry; that under the best conditions, if teaching institutions were what they should be, the university is the most natural place for the literary artist as well as the literary scholar."[61]

This important realization would influence the poet's future professional career, and it defines the kind of teaching he would

43

do. He cites other writers who were also in a general sense teachers: Dante, Milton, and T. S. Eliot. Again Ezra Pound seemed to him — "the kind of stimulus which could help bring about these better academic conditions: that he was in disrepute was only a result of his criticism of the present academic methods of teaching and interpreting literature, and the signs of change were everywhere abundant. Poets were moving into the universities."[62]

In this context Dudek admits that his essay "Academic Literature", published in *First Statement*, August 1944, would no longer be just a criticism of the teaching profession, since the structures in the universities have changed. Already in 1951 he wrote — "Where could one do more for poetry than in the place where it was being studied by the young and passed on from generation to generation? In the midst of 'young men' (Yeats) poetry could both be written and the way for poetry prepared."[63]

However, the demands of teaching and intense study left Dudek little time to write poetry during those years. "I find that a solid day goes to a new poem when other work demands immediate attention; but somehow the successful poem — successful in terms of oneself — is complete reward and satisfaction against anxiety."[64]

After completing the oral examinations for his doctorate, more time was available for Dudek to write poetry and meet with the young writers who gathered around Ezra Pound at St. Elizabeth's Hospital.

In 1951 Dudek accepted a teaching post at McGill University in Montreal, the most interesting part of his program "being a course in Modern English and American Poetry given in the Extension Department."[65] Thus began his long association with McGill. His wife had not completed her studies at Columbia so she remained in New York after Dudek returned to Montreal. He continued working on his dissertation: "The relation of printing history to literature,"[66] an area of perpetual interest to him, as we know from his own experiences in printing with *First Statement* magazine. He had completed a history MA: and his thesis had dealt with the profession of letters in the nineteenth century, a subject which now became specifically literary.

The 1951 Poetry Award of *Northern Review* went to Louis Dudek for a group of poems he had published in the magazine that year. At the same time a manuscript he sent to Ryerson Press was trimmed down to appear as the chap-book *The Searching Image*. Two poems in this book develop ideas we have seen first in the early poetry: the Greek aesthetic philosophy now becomes integrated with the process and the content of the poetry.

In "Acropolis" the poet's eye scans his one room apartment in New York, noting the many Greek reminders and allusions in the contemporary trivial world. From these Greek particulars his thought moves back in time to the golden past of Greek civilization: to the original freedom and beauty that survives despite the erosion of time and therefore is present in his room: "most Greek, is the air/ − unmarried to time − " (*SI*.7), he writes.

The second poem, "Line and Form," is more theoretical, yet it defines the poet's aesthetic philosophy with an extraordinary clarity of symbol and image. The complex interrelation of powers, or forces in nature produces the variety of complex realities which are the "mushrooms, elephants/ and women's legs" (*CP*.64) of the poem; or more simply, they are "a wind or the sky" making shapes by their mutual interaction.

But each power, alone, unentangled with others, would be infinite and eternal. The essential form of each is perfect in itself:

> Eternal forms.
> The single power, working alone
> rounds out a parabola
> that flies into the infinite; (*CP*.64)

So the shape of things in the world we know exists in the form of limitation. It is a compromise, consisting of many reconciled and partial possibilities realized.

> So this world of forms, having no scope for eternity,
> is created
> in the limitation of what would be complete and perfect,
> achieving virtue only
> by the justness of its compromises. (*CP*.64)

45

The poet's thoughts are set down in a form that flows as naturally as the elements he describes, and the aesthetic process now becomes, in itself, a subject in the poetry. As he has said in an earlier poem:

> The flame of a man's imagination should be
> organic with his body,
> coincident with an act, like an igniting spark.
> ("On Poetry" *CP*.24)

Again, Dudek's explanation of the biographical element in "The Black Girl and The Poem" (*SI*.5) is an example of how the poem is created by this method. The poet saw the beautiful girl on a bus, for only a moment. The real experience is not as significant here as the way the mind imagined that experience. It is this charge of life, ofttimes instantaneous, that provides the heat of creation (RC, Oct. 16/76):

> ...she had aroused
> the flame that now burned me, burned the poem out.
> Nothing mattered but
> her ebony body and eyes white as shell
> I could not have,
> which in the imagination stood perfected. (*SI*.5)

So it is the actual experience, but predominantly the experience as contained and perfected in the imagination, that is transformed to an aesthetic object, in this case, the poem.

There is a synaptic break between the ideal mental wish and the realistic event that precipitates the poem: "this is poetry, action unrealized:/what we want most we imagine most, ..." ("On Poetry" *CP*.24). Oscar Wilde wrote that (the second rate artist) "... lives the poetry that he cannot write. The others write the poetry that they dare not realize."[67] Dudek, following Wilde, uses his imagination to complete the synaptic response.

At this point, a new chapter in the poet's life begins. "The Fifties are crucial years in Dudek's career," writes Douglas Barbour, "because during them he wrote two long poems *Europe*

(1955), and *En Mexico* (1958). It was in these poems that he came into full command of his voice, and it was there that he truly became a philosophical poet."[68]

In the years ahead, also, he will bear the titles of poet, professor, editor, and critic, a period which may be defined as the midsummer of his professional career.

Dudek at the beginning of his career, *ca.* 1940.

Emilia Rozynska   Stanislaw Rozynski

Poet's grandparents, on the mother's side.

Poet with parents and sisters Irene and Lilian.

At Charlemagne, Quebec, early 1950's.
Back row: Lia Souster, John Sutherland, Stefanie and Louis Dudek.
Front: Raymond Souster
(photo: Raymond Souster)

Louis Dudek, Rapallo
in the background, 1953.

Louis Dudek, Roddick Gates,
McGill University, 1982.

(photo: Ian Stein)

Way's Mills, Quebec, July 22, 1978, photographed by Betty Gustafson.
Front: Louis Dudek, Avrum Malus, Aileen Collins, Ron Everson.
Middle: Monique Jones, A.J.M. Smith, D.G. Jones, Marion McCormick.
Back: Daryl Hine, Ralph Gustafson, John Glassco.

Chapter V

The Evolution of a Poetic Form

Dudek's concern with poetry in general, and his own poetry in particular, became a more serious program after he returned from New York to teach Literature at McGill University in Montreal. "My problem with poetry now is to find adequate form for an adult consideration of reality, one which excludes the romantic impulse to burst the bounds of what is simple and rational and commonplace. Reality is always strange and unfamiliar, ultimately "romantic" ... but one must arrive at it through the actual not by any exclusion of matters of fact." [69] He began a personal quest for a new and more appropriate poetic form. "The conflict between the commonplace and the strange, between the obvious and the incomprehensible, seems to offer material for poetry, for which one must find a form. I think this theme is really a continuation of something which has been recurring in my poetry and which is marked in this chap-book, *The Searching Image*." [70]

Dudek's poetry was appearing at this time in *Contact* and *Contemporary Verse*. This early poetry, says Frank Davey, "... consists almost entirely of short lyrics that derive a concluding insight or philosophical observation from the description of a particular scene or event. They contain little metaphor or literary image, depending instead on the evocative power that is innate within the names and qualities of physical phenomena." [71]

Invigorated by Ezra Pound's literary principles, on his return to Montreal, the young academic "... devoted his energies to reviving the experimental kind of alternate publishing that had been begun a few years before by Sutherland's *First Statement* and First Statement Press. His knowledge of the U.S. avant-garde and of its dependence on the editorial aggressions of such men as Pound and Corman had convinced him that the survival of a serious and creative Canadian poetry required that the poets have access to an alternate means of publication to that of commercial publishers."[72] Renewing contact with the Montreal literary group, Dudek promptly set out to encourage a new beginning in Canada to create a genuine school of modernism in poetry. John Sutherland's reaction against modern trends at this time resulted in a re-grouping of poets. Souster established *Contact* magazine in Toronto, and Layton and Dudek joined forces with him, sharing editorial responsibilities. Rather than rely solely on First Statement Press, they set up Contact Press, a small press which published *Cerberus* in 1952, the first book in a long series. "We fools made our poems as fast as feathers of snow," Dudek was to write much later in "Fragments 2" (*CP*.297). At the time, however, in the preface to Cerberus, Dudek described their philosophy: "We three in this book share the same affirmations and therefore the same negations in the face of the present. ... Our theme is love. But who can sing of love at the walls of Hiroshima, Belsen, Korea? ... Poetry, therefore, opposed to this, has power, immense power for good, because it is the true poem, the epic all men would live if they were free. And that is, after all, what we want."

As mentioned previously, in the poem "On Poetry" he asserts "that it is imagination − as poetry, faith, ethics − which gives order and beauty to life" (*C*.13). "Apparition" (*C*.30) and "Lovers" (*CP*.65) are two poems imaginatively conceived. "They came out of a level of consciousness," Dudek remarks, "that I know nothing about;" they were written spontaneously, in contrast to his previous conscious construction of verse. In future, the poet will return more and more to the method of creative production employed in these poems.

Dudek and Souster operated Contact Press from 1952 to 1967, publishing a group of poets, says Davey, that "... constitutes a history of the new Canadian poetry of the period – Dudek, Souster, Layton, Phyllis Webb, Eli Mandel, D. G. Jones, W. W. E. Ross, Alden Nowlan, Al Purdy, Milton Acorn, Gwendolyn MacEwen, George Bowering, Frank Davey, John Newlove, and Margaret Atwood."[73] Dudek's own continuing output of poetry, together with the stimulation of being in constant contact with other Canadian poets, results in a great sense of involvement during these years.

Michael Gnarowski recalls attending three literary parties Dudek hosted over the years – one on Beatty Street in Verdun, the second on Vendôme, Stephanie's home in Westmount, and the third at his current home on Ingleside. It was the third party in 1967, during "Expo", that Henry Miller attended, on his way back to London from California. Miller at this time, Gnarowski comments, "was an old man with an aura about him of intense serenity." Ezra Pound was to have attended this Expo conference but unfortunately he was ill.

In 1952 Contact Press published *Twenty-four Poems*, one poem for every hour of the day. One of these, "Pure Science," is valuable as a definition of the poetry-making process. For Dudek, poetry is "...a man-made kite/skating on an imaginary sky," and ultimately "a whirling/spark in a vacuum" (*CP*.151).

> Poetry is a man-made kite
>   skating on an imaginary sky,
> But nobody knows what the sky is
>   nor why there are kite-makers.
>
> It is also like grandmother's idea of heaven
>   that we have learned to do without
> Because nobody cooks there,
>   sleeps with girls, or mints money.
>
> It is a whirling
>   spark in a vacuum,
> And only scientists seem to
>   enjoy the experiment. (*CP*.151)

The literary techniques available to a poet and the free-flowing structure of the lines are now for him a more natural form than prose to describe the complex process of artistic creation – a preoccupation that will recur regularily in his poetry.

As with many poets, says Dudek, the conception and creation of a poem may take only a few minutes. This was the case with the poem "Emily Dickinson" (*TS*.112). Dudek was reviewing Dickinson's poetry just prior to giving a lecture, when the feeling overwhelmed him that Emily Dickinson had been so restricted and bound by her environment that she never realized her full human dimension – and yet her poetry, like an oak tree, belongs to the species of greatness. Perhaps during this period he, too, felt confined, having the desire to experience fuller life, so that he identified strongly with Emily Dickinson without being entirely aware of it. The tree, his old symbol, is now a metaphor for the poet. He took the poem into class and read it to the students, as an opening to the lecture – the epitome of modern poetry in action. As he says, it all happened within minutes.

> I saw an oak tree in a pot,
> It was a very pretty thing:
> Its branches had been often cut
> So that it kept its tiny plot.

> The narrow body twisted up
> And glistened in the frightening sun;
> Two feet of stem inside a cup –
> And yet an oak from root to top.

> Nature is great in filling space
> Tight as an atom with desire,
> But for a tree a room's no place;
> To put it there was a disgrace.

On the other hand, it can sometimes take years before an idea or image is formed and set onto paper, as we learn from "East of the City" (*CP*.33). Dudek attended Lansdowne Elementary School, an English Protestant school located on St. Catherine Street, near Delorimier, in Montreal's East End. Some of the images in stanzas one and two of this poem were implanted in the poet's mind when he was eleven years old. He used to sit in school gazing out of the window during class, watching the Jacques Car-

54

tier Bridge being built. Walking home after school he would pause to look at the new structure – "Between the knees of the bridge, crouching/By a wall..." (*CP*.33). This was the place where "East of the City" was first imagined in 1929; as a poem it was conceived in 1944, and finally completed in 1946. We can say that the "creative processing" occupied some seventeen years.

In 1953 Dudek and Layton became involved with a new little magazine *CIV/n* edited by Aileen Collins. In "The State of Canadian Poetry: 1954" Dudek explains the editorial position both of *CIV/n* and *Contact*. "Our underlying position in *Contact* (as well as in *CIV/n* the Montreal magazine) is one of sharp social criticism, but not a criticism based on political or economic grounds alone: it is a cultural attack, a criticism of contemporary life in the name of the whole range of liberal values; and the poetry that we make on this basis is as varied as the personalities of poets can be." [74]

Layton and Dudek became associated with *CIV/n* through Dudek's relative Stanley Rozynski, a sculptor, and his wife Wanda, who knew Aileen Collins and introduced her to the two poets in 1952. Aileen Collins wanted to bring out a little magazine and she invited Dudek and Layton to help her. The magazine was published on Bercy Street at the Rozynskis' home (*RC*, Mar. 15/77). "It followed Souster's mimeographed Toronto magazine *Contact* ... There was always a tactful solicitude on the part of Layton and myself not to interfere with the ... editors. We read the poetry before a group at Layton's house, enjoying free comments and debate over the poems, but we made no decisions ... It (*CIV/n*) was free-wheeling to a degree that neither Layton nor myself probably would have made it if we had edited it ourselves. On the whole it was lighter and less pretentious, and more fun, than any magazine I can remember." [75]

Dudek and Collins discovered they had common interests: a belief in providing an outlet for Canadian poets to publish their work, and a desire to produce and distribute this material. A friendship developed and in time a new strain emerged in Dudek's poetry.

During this period, Stephanie Dudek, the poet's wife, was studying at Columbia University in New York, while Dudek we

55

know, had returned to Montreal to teach at McGill University. In the summer of 1953 (*CIV/n* No. 3 had just been published) Louis and Stephanie decided to travel to Europe together.

The poem *Europe* records their travels and hence is by its nature biographical. It is Dudek's first, long, voyage poem. Both the form and content are innovative. The poet's voice is conversational, no longer masked by the authorial tone of his previous tightly structured verse. The wide background of knowledge that he has accumulated from studying and leisure reading is apparent in the poetry and is conveyed naturally in free verse. As he travels from city to city, the thoughts and associations he has are recorded as they occur in a seemingly spontaneous form.

There are some indications in *Europe*, however, that the Dudeks are at odds. "'Just a lot of water', someone says" (*CP*.83) is Stephanie dismissing the sea. The poet, however, idealizing and mythifying the sea, writes that "All that is good in us is still whatever of the sea/we contain." (*CP*.83)

Section 25 refers to his tentative relationship with Aileen Collins.

> Strange, that in the midst of all this deep-
> sea novelty and nonsense
> I think of someone far away
> at the end of the world
> where we started. (*CP*.86)

The phrase "where we started" is deliberately euphemistic. It might resonate as the emotional point where this new friendship began, or as the voyage itself, or as the city that the Dudeks left from on their voyage to Europe.

The Dudeks had been living apart in two different cities, leading different lives. Meeting Aileen Collins and working on the magazine complicated the poet's personal life. As a man who believes deeply in marriage, he found himself in a difficult position (*RC*, Nov. 5/75). It would, in fact, take seventeen years before these difficulties would be resolved — though some things are never fully resolved. This conflict is suggested by the sombre personal note that occasionally emerges in passages of *Europe*,[76] for example:

                              the enigma
           of our tortured lives cannot be answered
              by visiting an island. (*E*.51)

   In Rome Dudek received mail from Montreal. Letters from
Aileen Collins, Irving Layton, and Robert Currie. His feelings
come out in the text:

           Until these letters came I had not known
                 how far we had gone
           over the sea, the broken crags
           and ruins ...
           But you, sweet children of light, my friends,
                 whose letters come by post,
           are all earnest and alive,
           write, asking where I am, what I have seen,
           and make me know how lonely
           and isolated we have been among the ruins.
                           ...
           To be torn from these roots is to be dying. ...
                     (*Europe, CP*.109)

   In Section 44 of Europe Dudek writes. "One wants an
occupation that serves the world, not for cash but for the sake
of the work." (*E*.58)

He feels that the two most fruitful occupations of mankind are
teaching and pastoral preaching (*RC*, Nov. 5/75). His work as
poet and professor in a sense incorporates both, and it is perhaps
this combination that is responsible for the "Note" opposite the
title page of *Europe*: "As for being didactic, Plato teaches, at the
end of the Republic, that we had better be, if we want a place in
Utopia." (*E*.n.p.). This statement is the poet's ironic comment on
his didacticism in *Europe* – for the didacticism is related to the
Utopian vision. Yet it is didactic. The poetry is a means whereby
he can inform the reader about life, and in particular here about
Europe. It defines a moral responsibility. In Section 36 he writes
"Here you can sit and understand/how one building can civilize a
city" (*CP*.92). In other words he is saying: the ruins of past
civilization can point to a great future. Yet man destroys this

57

possibility: "Have I said enough/that wars destroy, not only the living bodies/but all the good that men create?" (*E*.131).

In *Europe* Dudek is speaking directly to the reader, something he has rarely, if ever, done before in his poetry. The voyage, which is a symbol of a human lifetime because it has a beginning, a middle, and an end, allows the poet to compare cities, artifacts and people. By doing this he believes that knowledge is increased: "Life, like poetry,/can only be understood through comparison," and "what results/is the perfect, unchanging essence,/an eidolon of the good." (*CP*.123).

Europe was written by "taking the actual, immediate experience, writing it down one or two days later, and then hammering and chiselling and polishing it to produce this prose-like thing where the words flow naturally" (*RC*, Nov. 5/75). The poet's vision here is "Not Catholic, but universal" (*CP*.99). His ideas are conveyed in an expository manner: personal, simple and straightforward. The poems are linked together as fragments of a large pattern. The change in the method of writing *Europe* is important because it is a precursor of the future from that Dudek's poetry will take.

In 1955 Dudek successfully completed his Doctorate in English and Comparative Literature. In the following year, reflecting that important poets had appeared at McGill in the past without a permanent record, he independently established and financed the McGill Poetry Series (though some poets paid for their own publication). Leonard Cohen, Daryl Hine, George Ellenbogen, Dave Solway, Seymour Mayne and Pierre Coupey are some of the writers brought out in this series. In total, ten books were brought out. The venture terminated in 1966 because the series was drifting from its original purpose, which was to publish only rare and genuine talent, and was becoming just another outlet for poetry on the campus. (*RC*, Feb. 10/77).

In 1956 *The Transparent Sea* was published by Contact Press. Unlike *Europe* (1954), most poems in this book are short verses, several written as early as 1942. However, in "Keewaydin Poems" (which won the University of Western Ontario Medal for poetry in 1956) and in "Provincetown," the serial free verse form attempted in *Europe* recurs. This book is of biographical significance because

58

in it one can trace the poet's maturing development with some clarity.

Dudek's description of himself in the 1950's is recorded in "No Answer":

> A woodpecker knocked on my skeleton
> And found it very hollow
> And very thin
> Where all my aching marrow
> And blood had been. (*CP*.159)

In the period from 1952 to 1955 he seems to have been concerned with thoughts of death and total emptiness — a feeling of loss that was intellectual as well as emotional (*RC*, Oct. 8/75).

In *The Transparent Sea* the love poetry shows him as active and positive. His passionate nature finds expression in poems such as "Virginal", "Lover to Lover," "The Creative Element," "Divine Touches", and "I Wrote it With Joy."

> The love I have in me comes rising in great waves
>   tossed at your mighty
> Small magnificent body, the floss of it
>   a heavy foam, tossed
> at your belly and shoulders till it overwhelms
>   you, I feel it overwhelms you,
> most beautifully, and makes an ocean around you.
>
> Kiss me, kiss me now in this element! This
>   is what they say started things,
> this is how they created whales and things
>   rolling it in a sea of storm,
> overwhelmed and swirling in the fertile fury
>   when the gods took chaos in hand.
>
>   (The Creative Element *TS*.71)

This happiness soon becomes clouded, however, and the painful process of loss discussed previously is evident in poems such as "Country Air" (*TS*.50), "Quarrel" (*CP*.71) and "Last Words" (*TS*.80).

We see that the green of the trees is Dudek's happy colour in the love poetry, and in "Another April" (*TS*.47) for example the colours the poet's mind sees during these years reflect his mental landscape. The girl in the green dress in this poem is not with him now and therefore there is a touch of sadness. Here the poet's eye, as a result, picks up and identifies with the grey tree, as well as the green memory (*TS*.47). So, too, the poem "Coming Together and Parting" records the poet's new awareness regarding the mutability of relationships. Dudek's relationship with Irving Layton, as well as with Stephanie tended to be somewhat turbulent at this time.

> Do not think that you will be loved forever,
> or keep a friend. They are yours
> only to use and lose –
> for exercise, mating and making,
> and recollection after
> in the fine anguish of loneliness. (*TS*.98)

This sense of mutability results in further contemplation of life and death. In Dudek's poetry death and life are not opposites but are parts of a greater whole. The poems often present the past juxtaposed with a change observed in the present. This change is a matter of coming to an accommodation with reality; a wearing down process which is precipitated by the poet's awareness that the erosion of Time, whose parent is Death, is a human condition. In "The Child," his most poignant poem on death, the poet portrays the young girl striking her fists against the tyrant death:

> The tripping of a girl just eight years old,
>   a skyward leaping
> up from the arches and the tiny thighs
>
> in swings, like flying –
>   springs with a laugh into living,
> up from the earth, from dying.
>
> Faustus, see
> Margaret at her leaping, reaching hands;
> she winds her wrists around
> with blue and strikes her fists
> against that tyrant who
>   in   a little time

will catch her at her skipping, in her sleep,
and stop all flying,
cover her with earth and down her bed
with small cold feathers from ungrieving skies. (*CP*.63)

There is a sense of tragic futility here, for Time and Death are inescapable and the child is no match for them. Death is further described as "...mindless death, ungenerous..." (*CP*.72) in the poem "On Sudden Death" written in memory of Walter Zuperko, Stephanie's father. *The Transparent Sea* covers the range of the poet's thought about death, from earlier poems such as "The Great As If" and "On Sudden Death," to the hope that after life we may be "bathed in a morning light of sudden gladness." ("The Dead" *CP*.73).

Another aspect of dark realism evident in this book is the living death that workers endure in an ill society. They are described by the poet going to their jobs, day by day, like animals — "Society their cage, in which they sit etherized and serve." Their week is waiting for Sunday, their one day of freedom ("Looking at Stenographers" *CP*.38). The capitalist employer is "an old rich idiot" like Scrooge, greedy and demanding ("Old City Sector" *CP*.37). The city, most often Montreal, is as black and dirty as Dickens' Coketown is in *Hard Times*.

This gut-end of a hungry city
costive with rock and curling ornament...

...

Later, enter the pinched clerks and the typists...

...

they work and wait for their simple Sundays,
for the evening show, or sex,
always in the grip and tension of this intestine,
the small capitalist's greedy space
where tight-fisted profit is squeezed out
in the torsions of crass inequity and private bitterness.

CP.37)

Effective use of consonants in the above lines serves to emphasize the poet's horror at such an oppressive existence.

Contamination of the environment is another form of death in *The Transparent Sea*. Visiting the ocean, Dudek describes how modern man has made the shore and the sea his litter barrel. This turbulent body that to him is a source always of poetic inspiration has been violated, so he writes:

> The problem
> was to reconcile the public beaches
> with the veritable Atlantic. *CP*.141).

In a personal aside (indicated by parentheses) he explodes with violent indignation as he will again and again, at the risk of the poetry:

> (whatever they touch
> is like them, these multi-arseholed
> mass-mindless Americans –
> because they've been here, the sand is filthy,
> the ocean trivial)
> (*CP*.141).

This has to be seen in the context of Dudek's idealistic vision and his determination to deliver reality. The paradox, however, is that the masses whom he champions at times are the very people who contribute to the vulgarity and inhumanity of our times; a fact perhaps less important to him at this point than the realization that their lives are prison terms. They are "caught up in a net" ("The Dead" *CP*.73) and "they die in gossamer cages their frail minds can never break." ("Looking at Stenographers" *CP*.38). The poet's vision of the worker is that he is "a feeble animal" (*CP*.30), mentally whipped and beaten, living in an "intestine" (*CP*.37) "like those/caged animals, born in captivity, who do not know/why they are unhappy." (*CP*.131).

The society that governs these people is depicted in "The Tolerant Trees" as one which celebrates "our puberty rites of golf and war" (*CP*.63). The rich dabble in golf and politics. At the time this poem was written the politicians of the world were playing a very sophisticated game of war. What makes society a living death, according to the poet, is war, murder and sport ("Keewaydin

Poems" 5, *CP*.136). Nature, in the meantime, preserves a menacing silence.

In *The Transparent Sea*, just as the senseless detruction of man is lamented, so too is the senseless destruction of Nature by man. Both are a source of grief. Man, who has to kill in war in order to survive, also must kill to subsist. But even more, something has gone awry, for –

> ... man, the top killer of them all,
> ... has brought three-quarters of the birds, fish, and animals close to extinction
> and now does his slaughtering systematically. ...
> ("Keewaydin Poems" 5, *CP*.136).

And yet the poet suggests that "tenderness is also a principle ... in our sad experience" ("Keewaydin Poems" 5, *CP*.137); and "we would have it all, all tenderness." But that is impossible. Unlike the "uncondescending trees," which are "too wise to speak against us" ("The Tolerant Trees" *CP*.63), the poet's intention here is to shock his readers out of a comfortable moral complacency. So that ultimately: "We must look for some new aesthetic of life which can bring seriousness and dignity to everyday affairs. We need new nobilities."[77]

At the same time, a preoccupation with the aesthetic of creating art is the subject of a group of Dudek's poems. "The Moment" reflects a new sense of total freedom, without assumptions, that has not appeared before in his poetry.

> The poet who begins to write no poem,
> he is the one I want to be.
> Having no need to give
> of himself, and not convinced others need
> or would, in any case, take
> it, he is free.
> A poet beginning just to be.
> How smooth, and clean,
> this thought appears to me!
> The table has been cleared, a piece
> of paper on it...I sit and laugh
> at the beauty of my white

freedom for the act —
reluctant to end,
in decision, this perfect thing.
You who are curious,
will have to wait and see!
(*CP*.69)

Dudek recalls that at this point writing poetry became for him
an activity in its own right, not needing to be justified by moral or
political relevance. He in fact refers to this new sense of freedom
as a turning point (*RC*, Oct. 8/75). He is now released from moral
obligation as from "the starch of reason/that's gripping the world
in cold formality" ("March Wind" *CP*.161); he is open to a new
awareness of the natural energy that can be found in existence, and
goes forward "to meet the lascivious summer" (*CP*.161), where
pleasure, love and beauty are possible and balance out with
despair. This sense of well-being affects the content and form of
his poetry. In "Taking Shape" he expresses an exhilaration in
creating that is likened to a bird in flight.

Taking shape
(wings)
of pigeons

make a temporary, a true
forever continued
perfection!

So everywhere
whatever moves, whatever settles
rises on feet, or wings
takes its shape;
ungrace is its undoing,
a fear to fall,
defection;

so consonants close
(wings!) in a whorl
of vowels —

the same
and different
birds in other trees. (*CP*.68-69)

Clearly, he stands confident in the creative power of poetry. Like the birds, he is one among many artists free of the traditional forms of expression, free to create the unique forms of modern art. These forms are adjusted to the process of nature.

The creation of the poem and its relation to the world are further considered in "Theory of Art," where the physiological eye is part of a complex metaphor. The artist's eye, or his mind and imagination, strives for the maximum comprehension of reality through a combination of selected images or ideas with a unified centre of interest. This centre of interest is the nucleus of the poem. And as the lens of the eye brings a large landscape into a small area of focus, so the poem condenses or compacts the world. The poet's "vision" is thus re-incarnated in the created work: "The poem is vision" (*TS*.40). It is microcosm, in other words, a 'light vision' epitomized, and this becomes a leitmotif in Dudek's poetry as he attempts in each poem to recreate

> The whole world, there in compendium, all
> its huge fragments
> a silent landscape, in the perfect O of the eye!
> (*TS*.41)

The fine perception of feeling encompassed with the poet's vision is witnessed in "Meditation Over a Wintry City":

> Stalked by disease and death, as all men are,
> drowned in the apparent chaos of these times,
> artists and scholars walk their quiet ways,
> echo the pain that other men should feel, and understand
> and make their voices heard as something seen,
> above all sound. (*CP*.32)

Yet for Dudek, it is not only pain that precipitates the creation of the poem; the poem is also created "...out of the pleasures of my trembling senses./...out of my desires I make a world to be loved." ("Keewaydin Poems" 7, *CP*.137). The total picture would include pleasure and pain, and all human experience, in a poetic paradigm.

It is in the poetry that he strives to depict the truth, whether of image or idea. His poetry is his credo, and his personal pride hangs on conveying a true 'light vision'. According to Dudek, Chaplin's "Limelight" is "the greatest film" because it epitomizes a life-long quest for truth, as well as the struggle to achieve art. Dudek's quest is similar –

> The poetry in it is what gets me.
> Literally the words:
>   'I must have truth! truth!'
>   ("Chaplin's 'Limelight'" *TS*.34)

By this time Dudek was involved in almost every aspect of the poetic process; from the conception of an idea, the conveying of that idea in the form of art, to submitting the finished product for publication, and then finally becoming an editor and a critic. His belief in poetry as the key to ultimate reality made these activities natural and desirable. The little magazines *First Statement* and *CIV/n* flourished under his enthusiastic and devoted labours. He believed in them. They provided "the setting where new poetry and new poets have their beginning."[78]

The experience gained in working with these little magazines prepared the way for *Delta*, a small magazine edited, published and printed by Dudek from 1957 to 1966. He describes these years as "the lonely years" (*RC*, Nov. 26/75). His relationship with Irving Layton had come to an explosive end: "the acquaintance that ended in slander" (*TS*.98). Layton's popularity in Canada had dramatically erupted and his friendship with Dudek became marred by the clash of their egos and their ideals. *Cataract* contains a shocking example of the unpleasant feelings that were publicly aired:

"Well, Louis, I'm no intellectual, as you know," Layton wrote in 1962 but "I also know what is dead or dying ... You, Louis, have been dying slowly for several years. I have watched the process with heartburn and gaspains; its final stages, with vomity disgust. Editing *Delta*, writing your assorted pooperies for the *Montreal Star* and *Culture*, you may deceive others about the actual state of your health, but these activities are the convulsive twitches of a dying poet ... what do you want, an angel to come down and piss in your ear, some Pegasus brine rubbed in between your shoulderblades, a toadeye laid on your testicles? ... Now as you pass, professors pick their noses less thoughtfully ... Bats pluck at your garments, ravens fly out of your armpits," Layton blubbered at him in print, naturally, for all the world to read. Dudek, finding this level of argument distasteful, disassociated himself from Layton and his followers. Alone, in 1957 he "bought a Chandler and Price platen press for $600 and printed some books and magazines" in his basement (*Dk*.40).

According to the artist, "Henry Miller too had a magazine called *Delta* in Paris; in fact, there are other meanings to the word ... a delta is a fertile place, the mouth of a river, where it gathers rich material ..."[80] The magazine would represent Dudek's position through his choice of material, and aid in furthering his ideas about Canadian poetry. Always interested in new poetry, he felt at this time that "there can never be too much poetry,"[81] and he stated this in an editorial he wrote for *Delta* magazine in October, 1957. "In short this will be something of a personal magazine, with an impersonal program. I take poetry to mean a special form of writing, rhythmic, whole, heated by imagination, but with no restrictions of subject or form placed upon it, and with the same vitality of interests that prose has: we must win back the ground we have lost to prose, and discover new ground. For this, we want scope, and air, and the help of youth. We want to act as a forum and an exhibition for some correctives to an old malady. We want to present examples of fresh experiment with poetry."[82]

Frank Davey comments that in *Delta* Dudek "attempted to keep Canadian writing within the international avant-garde community and encourage the socially-aware, realistic kind of writing he had always favoured."[83]

In 1957 Stephanie Dudek, having completed her studies in New York, returned to Montreal, taking a position in the Psychology Department at the Allan Memorial Institute. Their son, Gregory, was born on October 11, 1958. "Last night I read Genesis to Gregory,/'a bedtime story'" ("A Circle Tour ..." *CP*.317), the poet wrote a few years later. Now an adult, Gregory is a specialist in Computer Science in Toronto.

Europe 1954 marked the beginning of a distinct change in Dudek's poetry. "From 1942 to the time when I wrote *Europe*, I was becoming a public poet, ... The poetry had a certain amount of oratorical sweep, a certain confidence ... But I would say that I suffered some sort of defeat as a poet after that, and that I experienced a kind of withdrawal into myself as a result. Maybe it's even a good thing that it happened, that I became less rhetorical and more inward.''[84]

First, a personal and philosophical re-definition is evident in *The Transparent Sea* (1956); and in *Laughing Stalks* (1958) the satire and sharp criticism indicate that Dudek is now, as in *Europe*, the persona speaking out directly in his poetry. Then the 'lonely years' and "personal problems"[85] follow with a poetry of meditative withdrawal.

En Mexico, for example, is a record of the poet's concentrated meditations written while on vacation there in 1958. His mood is quiet, the content more philosophical. "There's another side to my poetry, an interest in ideas, in the philosophical content in poetry; and the philosophical, contemplative content probably runs counter to the concrete or imagistic. So there's an incompatibility. But I think you never get a great deal of contemplation in my poetry without seeing some pure images bobbing up, floating around in that element.''[86] The poem now is written at "a very personal introspective level ... I'm not addressing a crowd of people, ... but simply the visible creation, really just for myself.''[87]

In *En Mexico* the jungle, which has emerged from the sea, the central image of *Europe*, is a symbol of fertility, a place where vegetation becomes chaotic by the nature of its overgrowth. Realizing there is a fundamental truth embedded in the idea of the jungle, the poet's concern here is: "How the temple came out of the heart of cruelty,/and out of the jungle the singing birds!" (*CP*.206). He defines the new poetry as "the art of singular form – lines clean/as a wave-worn stone." (*CP*.212). This is the ultimate form for his poetry: he has come to believe that each new poem is a unique form generated out of the particular tensions in the mind and body (*RC*, Nov. 13/75), and each new poem is therefore "a signature of individuality, of integrity" (*CP*.213). This far-reaching conception of form in *En Mexico* is crucial, because it is here that Dudek realized that "Atlantis was in the cards – it had to be written" (*RC*, Nov. 13/75). There is an intellectual and imaginative concept evident here, affirmative of the creation:

> So praise the glory of the green jungle
> with all its terrible thunders;
> praise death and generation
> and the embracement of lovers under all skies. (*CP*.204)

However, an opposite current is also present. Dudek, in his forties now, felt his life flowing toward conclusion, toward death (*RC*, Nov. 13/75). So he also writes at the personal level, that "Optimism is foolish. Life can only be/tragic, no matter what its success." (*CP*.202) The way he attempts to deal with this opposing current is to "learn a stoic silence,/a little joy" (*CP*.209). In Mexico the poet finds relief from his problems: "There is no travail here,/no passion, pang, or impulse of despair." (*CP*.206)

"My own poetry had been snagged with personal problems, with illness and inevitable age, with the kind of questions I've been trying to investigate also. I've tried to make it come out of the real — to look into the actual and see what is there ... what is real."[88]

Personal depression and intellectual affirmation are the counterpoints that will continue in his life and work. The crux in *En Mexico* reveals again that Dudek is like those "Rootless flowers!/whose individuation is yet a part of their form ..." ("At Lac En Coeur" *CP*.217). In the following chapter we shall see how the same individuation will result in the creation of *Atlantis* and *Continuation I*.

Chapter VI

The Poetry of Maturity

Written in 1959, during a summer vacation in the Laurentians, "At Lac En Coeur" is a meditative poem (*CP*.214-219), an eleven-poem sequence in which the method of *Atlantis* is first attempted. Having developed a meditative sequential form for his poetry in *En Mexico*, Dudek is "Shaping a world already made/to a form that I require." In this poem, a solitary fir becomes the correlative for the poet — "(only by keeping apart from the others/can it assert that form)". He withdraws from society to be "Alone in the forest ... listening to the wind, looking through the pines," "feeling his way to the complex unities." He had realized in the jungle that "Silence is also a language" (*En Mexico, CP*.201); so here at Lac En Coeur he finds that it is "Perfect to live, alone, lonely,/ aspiring and self-fulfilled," growing like the tree, "... isolated/from the smothering multitude."

"Lac En Coeur," a short poem that follows, describes the act of writing "At Lac En Coeur." This short poem is important, since, as Dudek explains later, "the process of writing the poem, thinking the poem out, is now the important fact — I'm not arguing with the world anymore" (*RC*, Nov. 26/75):

> ... I wrote nothing
> I did not first think
> complete, as it stands.

Not a poem, but a meditation −
they make themselves, are also natural forms,
kernels that come whole to the hand. (*CP*.219)

"Lac En Coeur," then, marks the turning point where Dudek's writing becomes a true meditation, and therefore something like an automatic process. He will no longer compose verse to a set pattern but will have the poem assume an elastic form that appears naturally and automatically − "kernels that come whole to the hand" (*CP*.219) − generated by the thought process in the mind.

The field of psychology deals with the complex mental activity of thinking and forming thoughts: "... we know the world through our minds and our senses. This knowledge begins with perceived things, which later acquire meaning."[89] So in pursuing the sources of his later poetry Dudek turns to psychology. First, of this vast subject he writes ironically that "literature is a product of the mind, a peculiar by-product of the human psychological make-up. To find out what literature is, all you have to do is find out what life is all about and how we fit into it." It is more than we can expect to fathom. But then, "psychology is a half-science," he writes, "and we may get further with it than if we were to approach the problem through philosophy or theology, which don't seem to have much in the way of new insights to contribute to the enlightened modern mind."[90] The intellectual search for meaning that began in the poet's teens has moved from theology, to philosophy, and now for a time to psychology. This happens because the poetry itself has become a psychological process.

Dudek explains in "The Psychology of Literature" that "The source of every work of literature is in a human individual, and that individual in a particular state of mind and motivation ... I would say, from long experience and observation, ... that creativity is a crisis phenomenon. It is the result of problems facing the individual psyche − exactly as Freud explained the origin of dreams − and it is an attempt to resolve these problems in complex symbolic forms ... The crisis, of course, is internal; ... the first meaning of a poem ... is biographical: it comes out of the tensions and dilemmas in the mind of the author, and it is therefore a concrete symbolic representation of these tensions and dilemmas."[91]

The personal depression detected in *Europe* (1954), *The Transparent Sea* (1956), and *En Mexico* (1958) indicates that Dudek was suffering from "tensions and dilemmas." The unpleasant split with Layton; solitary production of Delta magazine; becoming a father in an unstable marriage; the death of his own father on July 31, 1959, all contributed to the poet's withdrawing into a more private poetry. Like the solitary pine, he feels that "To live" he must "become immune/to every bleeding cosmic wound" ("At Lac En Coeur" *CP*.217). Knowing that poetry is created by a complex process of thought, he writes now, recalling his ideas in the poem "Theory of Art," (*TS*.41) that:

> Anywhere the eyebeam transects the world, a thorn
> strikes with such sharpness to a thought.
>
> (*CP*.219)

These words may bring to mind Shelley's notorious line: "I fall upon the thorns of life! I bleed!"[92] It is a line Dudek likes to quote, half-ironically. In fact a "crisis phenomenon" had effected a change in the content and form of the poetry, apparent by the poet's self-concentration in "At Lac En Coeur."

Dudek has been described by his critics as a meditative and therefore a philosophical poet. This may in part be true, but in his poetry dating from the "Lac En Coeur" poems, he is a meditative and therefore psychological poet — a somewhat different case — because from this point on he attempts through poetic form to recreate "the real continuous process of poetry-making that goes on in the mind."[93]

During a sabbatical leave in 1961, Dudek sailed to Europe, his destination Naples, Rome, Florence, Paris and London. A long poem, later called *Atlantis*, was proposed in advance as his project for this voyage. "I undertook to write a poem — to bring together the serious and the human in a speaking voice — kinetic words filled with an energy" (*RC*, Nov. 26/75).

Atlantis is the most ambitious undertaking Dudek has attempted in his poetry. It is an interior monologue in free verse, continuing the method of "At Lac En Coeur." "I worked on this poem for six years to give it order and coherence, music and form" (*RC*, Nov. 26/75). Musing, years later, about this shift he said that "What happened actually to my poetry, you see, is that it took a direction evolving out of itself ... namely, toward a fragmentary and continuing process of meditation and creation ... recording the words that come to you and writing them down continually in a book, and then reworking them – ... Usually cutting out, rephrasing slightly; I have a respect for divine dictation."[94] In the prologue part of *Atlantis* he plays variations on the idea of unique poetic expression, "the art of singular form" (*En Mexico, CP.*212):

> And it would be far more difficult, almost impossible,
> to write a poem in the rhythm of another, earlier poem
> than to write a new one, in the rhythm of a new one.
> (*CP.*228)

The purpose of the voyage is to contain life in a metaphor, and so attain the universal:

> Travel is the life-voyage in little,
>   a poem, a fiction, a structure of illusion!
> ...
> Travel, to and from (the place does not matter)
>   the Ding an sich in a mirror –
> Let it speak! (*CP.*223)

Paradoxically, the "life voyage", which is "a structure of illusion," is at the same time the "Ding an sich" or thing-in-itself and the correlative for Atlantis. In the poem, it becomes the reality beyond reality, wherein the ultimate unknown is sought. The voyage is a metaphor that signifies the poet's quest to translate life into poetry, seeking the transcendent so far as it is knowable to man. The poet

> ... looks with warm detachment
>   out upon the world,
> and would create, out of that fury and violence,
>   an order and a beauty that is all his own. (*A.*83)

In an interview Dudek defined the Atlantis idea: "Atlantis – ... the mythological or symbolic word that contains what I'm talking about — It isn't visible in any concrete way — it isn't even in our lives; you don't see glory or heaven anywhere, you don't see God or transcendence ... But there is something going on, in the actual (it's in great works of art that I see for a moment what I'm looking for in that poem) ... In the poem I'm looking mainly at people in streets, in restaurants, in hotels ... I'm trying to understand what it is that has value and meaning, to rebuild the other half of possible existence."[95]

Dudek's belief is that "Atlantis,/ ... is our true home." (*CP*.230). He says: "Here nothing is real, only a few/actions, or words,/bits of Atlantis, are real./ ... in moments of illumination." (*CP*.231). Earlier, the poet had said that "one measures happiness in life on a scale of only moments" (that is, mere moments of happiness); now he describes this moment as the "Ding an sich" which is the ultimate reality. It is formed in "a pure perception" (*CP*.249), where all ideas and meanings start. His best expression of the Atlantis ideal is a 'light vision' that comes to him in these exceptional moments: "Like a long thought, a sweet remembering without words./ All-over light everywhere." (*CP*.249). And for the poet "... the visible world seemed to be waiting,/... to be revealed." (*A*.70).

The psychological process in the poet's mind which enables him to express the idea of Atlantis is a kind of vision, or revelation, about the nature of reality:

> What is it that a poet knows
> that tells him — 'this is real'?
>
> Some revelation, a gift of sight,
> granted through an effort of the mind —
> of infinite delight. (*A*.70)

The solitude of the poet allows him occasionally to hear "... the real world whispering/with an indistinct and liquid rustling — /as if to free, at last, an inextricable meaning!" (*A*.70). The poetry-making process, first intuited in *En Mexico*, is fully explored in *Atlantis*. In the earlier poem, obsessed with the idea of creating the ultimate art, he had "Sought for words, simpler, smoother, more clean than any," (*A*.70) but in *Atlantis* this verbal lucidity is an element in which we see the passing reality, like a world in water.

By this method the poet reveals the divine as the actual, always before us (*RC*, Dec. 10/75): "the visible world." And it is from this that possible wisdom comes, because like the past, like all deeply hidden truth –

> Unless we can see it live, it is a deep unknown – an Id
> that may strangle us in our sleep. (*A*.25)

Dudek clearly felt a spiritual power on this voyage, such that he actually speaks of the poetry as inspired by an "Angel of Poetry" (*RC*, Nov. 26/75). This is the ancient idea of inspiration as experienced for example by the Kabbalists; Milton claimed to be divinely inspired when he wrote *Paradise Lost*. More recently and closer to home, F. R. Scott has spoken of poetry in this way.[96] Dudek stresses, however, that his angel is not a poetic device, but rather a necessary correlative of the Atlantis ideal (*RC*, Nov. 26/75) –

> (The Angel of Poetry
>   must be different from any other angel
> – of sex, or war (*A*.23).

Yet "Angels leave only strips of cloud" (*A*.59), he observes, and these are the lines that have to be worked up in a finished poem. When the voyage ends, his Angel leaves him:

> I see my angel, flying over the water,
> to the blue that's like a thin gas flame around the world.
> Leave me, I said,
>   spirit that must rise above today and tomorrow.
>   (*CP*.284)

This poet, who began "walking full of poems" (*CP*.13), has moved to a level of high reflective awareness that most people never conceive of. He recognizes that the public response to the poem may be a disappointment to him:

> Already I hear
>   the creatures are laughing at my words.
> No one understands. It does not interest them. (*A*.149)

Regardless, he writes out of a creative process that flows on, like the creation:

76

I believe that the poem has a generative form
    like coral or hurricane.
Every white detail must be employed.
    ...
The infinite clarity when it began
    (if it began)
divided itself in space and time
    an infinite world of infinite worlds. (*A*.29)

To the artist, "Every energy is an angel" (*A*.47), therefore the poetry comes naturally and flows from deep sources. "An ecstacy after an ecstacy/to the quiet mind" (*CP*.323). He takes "what is distilled of transcendence/out of the visible" (*A*.135) and records "Eidolons, visions of that reality" (*A*.11). Recognizing that "It's hard to make a good book/that a young man might enjoy over his lunch/sixty years later..." (*A*.95), as an artist he has a responsibility to set down his interpretation of contemporary life.

    ... since there will be others after us
        ...
it is important that they should not be lost;
that we discover, add to, do whatever helps
    to enlighten them,

to find, in the initial darkness,
    – what, if not the final reality? (*A*.90)

In the early poem "A White Paper" Dudek had used a geological metaphor to describe the immortality of a poem. At the Redpath Museum of Natural History at McGill he had gazed long at a trilobite, and later he converted this stone fossil into the symbol for a poem. The trilobite fossil, once a living thing, has retained its shape and form over the aeons of time: so also the poem becomes a permanent record of living man:

    So you be a record of me ...
    that someone time hence
    may lift like a layer, and see
    me, white in the sunlight. (*EC*.12)

The same metaphor recurs in Atlantis, where the poem is compared to a piece of coral. Here the coral (which also once was alive and now has become an imperishable substance), represents poetry.

> These corals are excellent samples
> the end, perhaps, of long searching and care. (A.6)
> ...
> The search for meaning's a sudden compacting
> of thought that took maybe days or years –
> the poem a crystal
> formed in an empty cave of time. (A.7)

Art is made, Dudek says, when the particulars of experience and the concept-structures of the poet's mind compress reality into paradigms of existence and communicate these in the form of artistic fiction.[97]

As I see it, by creating the poem from the reality he perceives, Dudek creates a 'light vision' where the form and the body, like the coral, become an immutable structure defined as Art. What the poet wants "in art, as life, is the numinous present." (A.106) On the other hand this is the truth that will transcend time and become a record for future civilizations, and on the other it is "only a translation" (A.83) of life. Ultimately,

> ... we don't
> really matter that much. The permanent matters.
> Something that art reveals. (A.106)

As far back as 1951, in a letter to Dr. Lorne Pierce of Ryerson Press, Dudek explained his goal: "I have tried to write poems that contain honest and pressing ideas, that have variety and technical finish, that have both novelty and solidity which I hope will keep them from becoming trivial in two or three years."[98]

At the same time, Dudek believes that a good poem, like the living body, flows rhythmically together:

> A poem is like a living animal.
> If you look at any poem really close
> you will discover its anatomy.

Under the skin are veins, tendons, nerves
that move and hold it together. (*A*.24)

Unlike the perishable body, however, the poem is a permanent art
form; it is unchanging and eternal — "a piece of eternity."

Dorothy Livesay analyzed Dudek's work from a rhythmic or
metrical viewpoint in "The Sculpture of Poetry," 1966. She sug-
gested that the total effect of a Dudek poem is "kinaesthetic," ...
"an identification with the object seen and its flow". "His rhythm
is welded to the thought"; and there is usually a "conceptual con-
clusion"[99], central to Dudek's theme of mankind finding har-
mony and order in a chaotic world. After reading her essay,
Dudek wrote Dorothy: "Your essay is simply astonishing to me: it
is so exactly the heart of the matter, and I had given up hope of
finding a critic, or even a reader, who would see just this. When I
do a poetry reading ... I always say at the beginning that I would
like people to forget my ideas, and not to pay attention to what the
poems are saying, but for this time to listen to the sound, the shape
and rhythmic movement of the words, from line to line, and the
form they make. Then, if possible, to breathe the aroma, which
comes from this sound and rhythm, and which is the true poetry.
But alone, all this would be powder-puff poetry ... One thinks of
meaning, looks for images, and then with luck, the sudden stroke,
comes upon words and rhythms — one line will do — that are the
whole poem or the beginning of a poem ... But with my poetry,
this (essay) is just what was needed, to show the reader how it is
different, and how it may lead to new possibilities."[100]

Michael Gnarowski remembers visiting Dudek at his place on
Dorchester Street, then a bohemian section in Montreal, where
Dudek would read parts of *Atlantis* to him. Sheets of the poem
were pinned up on the walls — an assemblage of ideas in chunks
like collages.

In *Atlantis* Dudek comes to terms not only with total self but
also the many complexities of life. His full sensibility has poured
through the lines. Then in 1961 he travelled to the west coast to
teach a summer course at the University of British Columbia.
"Canada: Interim Report" was written on the return trip by train,
and Dudek's comment on the poem reveals just how much of

himself he had put into *Atlantis*, how much hope and subsequent disappointment this involved: "After *Atlantis* comes this despairing bloody poem. After *Atlantis* it was hard to live ... I had to face up to dying and other people's deficiencies" (*RC*, Nov. 30/76).

In *Atlantis* he had written how music allows the poet to escape the tensions and dilemmas of his personal life.

> At the height of great music
> (whether Puccini or Bach)
> one forgets the meaning, the lovers,
> the loss, even one's own tragedy... (*A*.28)

The biographical reference here is to Puccini's *Madame Butterfly*, a private association about his marital situation. As regards "one's own tragedy," in 1967 (the year *Atlantis* appeared) Dudek's marriage broke up finally — "(a broken marriage)/or happiness?" (*CP*. 323) and three years later, on October 18, 1970, at the Unitarian Church in Montreal the poet was married to Aileen Collins, former editor of *CIV/n*, now co-ordinator of high school English studies at the Montreal Catholic School Commission. The idea of a perfect marriage, however, had been celebrated earlier in the poem "Marriage."

> Tomorrow we join in marriage
> with ring and sweet song
> and the tears of the old.
> When we die our dusts scatter;
> but where we have loved so
> no gods need recall. (*CP*.161)

In "Les Répétitions" Dudek writes what he calls a true love poem of this period (*RC*, Nov. 26/76). A complex poem of 30 lines, it reads in part:

> What you give some men never get
> not in a lifetime of looking —
> the difference
> between sex and no sex
> is that between your speaking body
> and any other woman. (*CP*.292)

"All I ever wanted to say about love," he recalls, "is in this one poem" — the French title means "The Rehearsals" or repetitions of love (*RC*, Nov. 26/76). It contains deliberate subtleties that remain beyond the grasp of the merely casual reader.

During these years a change occurred also in the poet's literary life: "On the termination of Contact Press in 1967, Dudek transformed Delta into another small press, Delta Canada, which has published ... *Collected Poetry*."[101] Delta Canada was edited jointly by Louis Dudek, Michael Gnarowski and Glen Siebrasse; it published 32 titles between the years 1965 and 1971. Dudek's next enterprise was DC Books, a small press which brought out eight titles between 1971 and 1981. According to John Robert Colombo, *Collected Poetry* (1971) "includes many poems that no historical anthology of Canadian writing should be without. The *Collected Poetry* is something of a table that charts the drift of Western art from the 1940's to the 1970's — from very formal poetry to very open poetry, from private views of inner realities to more public and inclusive panoramas of culture and civilization."[102]

Finally, Dudek's feelings about Canada and his city Montreal are revealed in the poetry. Only by leaving his home — "'I hate travel'/but all the poetry I've ever written seems to be about travel," (*A*.9) — was he able to realize the virtues of America against the background of European civilization. On his first return from Europe he wrote:

It seems that we have come all this distance
to discover the virtues of America (the continent, Canada
being a good part of it) (*Europe, CP*.117)

It is not a flag he carries, but rather a sense of possibility regarding the Canadian future. Like Ulysses, to whom he relates himself, Dudek returns to Ithaca, "a country with certain resources,/and a mind of its own" (*Europe, CP*.119, 125). Freedom is a right of each Canadian in this democratic country, so that in the conclusion to *En Mexico* the poet is thinking also of Canada (*RC*, Nov. 13/75) when he writes: "Mexico, there, lies simple and bare — /strange as life anywhere" — and "Wherever you are, begin!" — (*CP*.213) because between the jungle and Atlantis lies

81

the real world, this world, and Canada, like life anywhere, is also teeming with potential and opportunity.

Dudek is highly critical of Canada when he is writing from within the country. It is part of his role as a culture critic. He imagines a people like the Greeks who might create great things and think great thoughts, but he finds only inert Canadians who are like Gogol's "Dead Souls" (*CP*.306). Somewhat desperately he says, "Maybe a revolution will save us" in "Canada: Interim Report". He quotes Voltaire: "'The Canadian savage persists,'" (*CP*.306) and he remembers lines from a poem by Raymond Souster: "What is it / that we're 'such second-rate sons-of-bitches'?" (*CP*.306)

As for the writer in Canada, he is faced with a public who reads little: "'Just because it's a book,/do I have to read it?'" * they ask. But Dudek's entire criticism turns on this issue: "How I believe in the book!/That it should perdure ... and grow/and that we be there:/the artist somewhere in the middle." (*CP*.310) In Canada the artist is "semi-developed," (*CP*.312) unlike the business man, who, having "replaced the warrior and the aristocrat" (*CP*.309) runs a truculent society without art, "Where money talks – a refined language." (*CP*.188) As Dudek sees it, Canada is a cultural wasteland – "O pioneers!/ ... You see what a mess we've made of it". (*CP*.312)

A poet who hates travel, yet by travel puts his homeland in perspective, he sees much room for improvement in his own country. "We live in the most-possible-of-the-best of worlds ... Also of the worst *per contra*" (*CP*.318) so that what we do matters. Through his satirical verse Dudek hopes to awaken the reader to a world of possibilities because there is "all the future ... a new beginning" (*CP*.285) – a new life and light. Moreover, "everything men hold to is what the voyager leaves behind" (*A*.141) – and there is something far more important in life than material acquisition. "'Look for it in your solar calendar'," he says: "Everything, whatever it is, is a kind of Canada." (*CP*.313) And since we are the creative species –

---

* *"Canada: Interim Report"* CP.307.

It all comes down to this life of ours
of which you have the pieces
   right in your hands. (*CP*.278)

In connection with national affinities one must mention also his attachment to French Canada. His home is Montreal.

Ruled by its ten percent of English ...
Where money talks − a refined language
And French bombs explode ...

    ...

Second largest English-speaking French city in the world
        ("O Montreal" *CP*.188).

Growing up among French Canadians in east-end Montreal, Dudek learned French naturally, understood and appreciated French culture, and felt himself enriched by it. Later, he read authors such as Proust, Mauriac and Gide. He took advantage of "French radio, newspapers, books, available so easily in Montreal."[103]

Recurrent evidence of the French influence is found in his work. In an essay written in 1964 he says: "I want to see French culture here enriched, strengthened, brought within reach of more young people. I am all for two languages in education (on both sides), and the widest cultural awareness."

"Unilingualism, on the other hand, I consider a misguided and ignorant prejudice ... separatism, would destroy all the good things that a complex relationship offers ... − openness to the English continent, fearless bilingualism − is what French Canada needs."[104]

A number of poems over the years refer to French Canada: "Patates au Four,"[105] "Les Innocents,"[106] "Advanced French,"[107] poems No. 5 and No. 9 from *Europe*; also "Two Nations" (*LS*.47), "The Biggest Turnips" (*LS*.48), "Radio" (*LS*.49), "La Parade" (*LS*.50), and especially Section II, part I of *Atlantis* which deals with France. There is also an unpublished, uncollected early love lyric "Pour Fernande," written in French for a French Canadian girl. From an early time Dudek has translated Emile Nelligan's poetry,[108] and he has returned to Nelligan in recent years (see *Tamarack Review*). He has written several critical articles which show his deep and long-lasting concern with the question of the two literate cultures in Quebec. In all of these articles he sees the promise of a rich culture composed of the two language-literatures of Canada as an opportunity missed and as an invitation always waiting before us. [109]

The great mistake of my life was to assume
that literary understanding and intellectual achievement
are a matter of choice and will, whereas they are a matter of
inborn character and endowment. Unfortunately, it's too late
to correct it; and I cannot adjust my sights to the
more humane and pessimistic perspective.
L. D.

Chapter VII

CONCLUSION

The writing of poetry is the be all and end all of this poet's existence as he strives constantly to project his central conception in numerous ways: the result is "the one good line in a poem" (*E*.93) or the one good poem among several. In 1982, he is all of the mind that the writing is sufficient unto itself. The experience of creating is in itself a fulfilment (*RC*, Feb. 10/82). "Continuation 1" is a poem that will possibly be his final ongoing poem, for he has subtitled it "An Infinite Poem in Progress." In this work one observes the poet combining lyrical fragments and setting them into a continous form that has the permanence of finished poetry:

> But to accumulate lines, is not that a pleasure?
> To weave them into patterns,
>   is not that happiness?
>   ("Continuation 1' *CP*.324)

These lines are a conscious parody, "a loving imitation" as he says, of Ezra Pound's lines in *The Cantos*:

> To study with the white wings of time passing
>   is not that our delight
> to have friends come from far countries
>   is not that pleasure
> nor to care that we are untrumpeted? [110]

The idea for "Continuation 1" came to him while he was still writing *Atlantis* in 1961:

I said to my friend, "Don't read this,
   it'll make you dizzy."
But she read on, said she couldn't stop.
   "What is it?"
I said: "The vertigo of freedom."
Why stop at all, she said, why not go on?
"Of course I can't stop," I said. (*CP*.274-275)

These lines, he says, are an imaginary conversation with Aileen. They are certainly a promise of things to come in the poetry. (*RC*, Sept. 30/75).

As Dudek sees it, the audience is not a necessary part of the writing of poetry; however, he seems to vacillate on this question from time to time. He says that he writes because the poetry comes to him and he writes it for no one but himself; (*RC*, Oct. 8/75) yet he also admits at times that poetry is for the world, hoping that the work will be read. Through poetry, he shows a man struggling through difficulties and disappointments, and further he offers to focus and guide our existence toward Atlantis (*RC*, Sept. 23/76). He fluctuates between a personal purpose and a highly didactic one. He believes that literature is ultimately moral. There are, of course, poems he writes but does not intend to publish, because they have not been carried beyond the primary level of reference, the biographical; he feels that the intimate details of life are not satisfactory subject matter for poetry unless they can be raised to universal significance. A poem in its first hand-written draft springs, he says, from an obscure inner impulse. Later, when it is worked up into a finished poem, if it is worth the labour, it becomes a poem in its own right, in the public domain (*RC*, Nov. 12/6). The transition from the first to the second stage is continuous and gradual, from the moment of conception to the completion of the poem.

Dudek's current attitude about publication of further sections of the "Continuation" poem is almost unconcerned: "When I feel that people want to read it," he says, "I will perhaps publish more," (*RC*, Sept. 23/76). So far, five sections have appeared in the book *Continuation 1* (Véhicule Press, Montreal, 1981). He believes that —

> All good poems
> are conversations with God
> and there is never any hurry
> to publish.
> (*CP*.326)

This may be a self-protective attitude; perhaps because of his own forthright criticism, he has met with much resistance and neglect over the years. The Governor General's Awards have passed him by and he did not receive a very enthusiastic response for his *Collected Poetry* in 1971 (in his own city neither of the English newspapers reviewed it), yet he does have a small body of devoted readers and critics, who happen to be some of Canada's best writers. Michael Gnarowski recalls that Dudek was writing serious and valid criticism yet the literary establishment chose at that time to ignore it. These *Selected Essays and Criticism* have since been compiled and published in 1978 by The Tecumseh Press and are an important commentary on contemporary Canadian literature.

John Robert Colombo, for example, says that "Louis Dudek, the Montreal poet and professor, may not be the best known poet in the country but his work certainly ranks with that of the best and it is ... the most interesting being written in Canada today."[111]

One recalls his lines in *The Transparent Sea* (1956) "... Don't forget/that failure-hurts ..." The artist's "worst dream", he then wrote, recalling Chaplin's "Limelight", "is an empty theatre."

More recently, in *Epigrams*, rather bitterly he says: "In a country like Canada where nobody reads, literary reputation is mostly based on rumour." (*Ep*. 24). And in *Atlantis:*

> I once wrote to Ezra, "If they explain your poem
> they'll kill it."
> He answered, "Don't worry. They won't." (*A*.130)

89

These observations apply to Dudek's poetry also, with its complex network of reference. Just as many artists have been misunderstood and neglected during their lifetime, one foresees that the important contribution of this poet to Canadian letters will be recognized in time.

In fact the literary community is already beginning to react. The summer 1976 issue of *Tamarack Review* was devoted to Dudek's work, as well as the double issue of *Open Letter* (Spring and Summer 1981) – these stand as a celebration of the artist and are a tribute to his worth. The critical study by Frank Davey, *Louis Dudek and Raymond Souster* (1981), as well as the present *Biographical Introduction* begin a new phase in Dudek appreciation and criticism. A *Check List* of his writings by Karol Wenek (1975) exists together with Dudek's *Selected Essays and Criticism* (1978) and the book *Technology and Culture* (1979). Various collections of unpublished writing are in preparation.

In 1975 Dudek published a collection of *Epigrams*, and in 1981 several important books appeared: *Cross-Section, Poems 1940-1980, Poems From Atlantis*, and *Continuation 1*, along with the critical dialogue, *Louis Dudek and the Vehicule Poets*. 1983 has seen the publication of his book *Ideas for Poetry* by Véhicule Press carrying a dedication which reads: *"For Aileen – an audience of one"*. He was awarded an Honorary Doctor of Letters at York University in June, 1983 and in December, 1983 he was appointed an officer of the Order of Canada.

Dudek holds the distinguished Greenshields Chair of English at McGill University. He is currently on sabbatical leave and approaches retirement in 1984 when he will, for the first time, devote himself entirely to writing poetry. He is occupied with the Continuation project, he says, because "separate individual short poems are not the form one wants. How much more interesting if one could document the real continual process of poetry-making that goes on inside the mind ... this real process instead of the artificial poem construction."[112] Consistent throughout the years has been his search for greater understanding of "the poetry-making process."

"The subject of my poetry now, I would say, as always, is the process of poetry itself, to ask what it is that the mind is doing to experience and to reality, what we are, and what the whole context of life is between eternity and the present. This is absolutely fundamental, and it's always manifested in terms of the things you see and hear and live with − the realities before you. The rest is speculation ... The main thing is the notion that there is a mystery contained in this human existence ... it is entirely illusory ... this whole life of ours will be wiped out ... when we die. Therefore, 'what is it?' This is the constant question before me ..."[113]

In 1956 Dudek published "The Great As If (*CP*.70). He returns again to this theme in "A Circle Tour of the Rockies."

> But then, in the end, we sleep
> (withdrawn from circulation)
> and the world goes on, building and dismembering
> its mountains:
> the great small enterprise where we have a ticket
> for only one ride −
> The Circle Tour. (*CP*.320)

Life is at once both microcosm and macrocosm, as seen here in the use of the oxymoron "great small." It implies our relative insignificance in cosmological and geological terms, yet our potential greatness in philosophical and psychological terms. It is a "Circle Tour" because whence we come, we must return.

> Not an uneventful voyage.
> Those who survive
> will have enjoyed the ride.
>
> Perhaps we die
> in order to make room for others. (*CP*.205)

The poet-philosopher, and teacher, concludes with practical remarks on the poetic profession, a theme which always concerns him: "... that I am perhaps different from other Canadian poets, in that it's not enough for me just to write poetry. I have an obsessive sense of vocation and of commitment to other poets, young poets − both the poetic activity and the critical activity.

What I want is a society of people who talk intelligently together about poetry, and look at each other's poetry, and help one another, and publish good poetry – a truly enlightened literary environment."[114]

Frank Davey has assessed Louis Dudek's contribution in striking superlatives: "Louis Dudek has had the most influence on subsequent generations of Canadian poetry of any poet in Canadian literary history. His lyrics, that build from anecdote or observation to a punchline of humour or philosophy, have provided one of the commonest structures in recent Canadian verse, being evident in the work of Al Purdy, George Bowering, Seymour Mayne, Michael Ondaatje, Lionel Kearns, Alden Nowlan, John Newlove, to name only a few. His work with the structure of the long meditational poem has marked the beginning of a period in which widespread experiment in this form has been one of the unique characteristics of Canadian poetry. Notable among those following Dudek's lead here, although usually without his didacticism, have been Bowering, Victor Coleman, Daphne Marlatt, Frank Davey, bp Nichol, and Dennis Lee."[115]

In a recent discussion Dudek remarked that the lifetime of an artist is only a small part of his total relation with the world (*RC*, Feb. 10/77). As a poet, however, he has attempted –

> To die undyingly. To say the word
> that echoes through time:
> to make the stars hear. ("Meditation ..." *CP*.30)

That Dudek is a thinking poet, a poet of important ideas, not an abstract writer, is reinforced by Michael Gnarowski, one of Dudek's first students at McGill in the 50's: "Louis invited us to think with him."

Anyone who has seen Dudek teach is familiar with this curious process. Tossing ideas like petals of a flower at his students, he would invite their comments, listening carefully. There would then be silence while the class would process this knowledge. He showed them, by his example, how to think on a deeper level. In his creaking old swivel chair at McGill, Dudek would tilt back, somewhat precariously, hands folded behind his neck, bite at the corner of his bottom lip, tap his foot, or rythmically swing his knee back and forth, lost in thought. Then he would quietly explain his theory, simple words of depth intricately woven with references and cross references that would astound the class. If anyone expressed amazement at his wide learning he would immediately become self-effacing. He belongs to a moralistic, puritanical, careful, non-extravagant ethos – a quiet, gentle man, unlike many writers who require more publicity than they have humility.

Shelley's "Ode to the West Wind" is one of Dudek's preferred poems from his high school days. Visiting Europe, years later, he passed the house where Shelley wrote the poem. "I passed the house where Shelley wrote 'The West Wind' (A.59) – the line found in *Atlantis* somewhat jars the flow of the poem at this point. It seems to be a random fragment. Other real life incidents also conflict with the artistic eternality of the poem – a problem the poet himself deals with regularly as he edits his work. Indeed, the poem is, on occasion, excessively autobiographical; irrelevant fragments of the literal world seem to be thrown into the artistic mix. So the relation of art to fact is a subject that not only the poet has dealt with but one that we have followed in this Biographical Introduction. The facts are that Louis Dudek, son of an immigrant, has travelled to Europe – and to the world of civilization – from the east-end of Montreal, from "That old world that could have suffocated you" (RC, Feb. 17/75). There is a mixture of humility and wonder that the poet always conveys in discussions about his past, which may not be readily apparent to the casual reader of his poetry. The past is magical and secret, the beginning of a long voyage. It must be explained, as the present must be explained. Dudek recently talked about his past in an interview with Michael Darling: "... coming from the east end of Montreal, I have a kind of aspiration towards the higher culture of the west end of this city, the English culture; and then having matured, this archetypal pattern ... the imprint of this aspiration of the proletarian to the higher culture, becomes transferred as the Canadian or American hankering towards the higher culture of Europe or the arts. This is probably just a humorous way of putting it.[116]

In the poem "Continuation 1" Dudek writes, though not primarily of himself, "For some have achieved while others suffer" (*CP*.323). He has surmounted considerable odds: ill health, the Great Depression, poverty and the costs of education before the period of grants, a very demanding teaching career, in addition to work in poetry and publishing. His goals were achieved by unusual perseverance. He admits that his working-class background could have been a trap – and adds that it very nearly was. One important consideration, however, is that even though he was aware of great obstacles, Dudek did not consider success at any time as a goal. And yet he is grateful and conscious of a considerable achievement, as scholar and teacher, as critic, editor, publisher – and as a poet.

INTERVIEWS

Interview with Leonard Cohen

*Best known of all Canadian poets, Leonard Cohen is admired widely as a novelist, poet, singer and composer. In the fifties, he was seldom seen without his guitar and his song **Susanne** has since received international acclaim. He is involved with Irving Layton in a Toronto-based venture called Charisma Publishing. Currently, his livelihood is derived mainly from the extended concert tours he embarks on during the winters in Europe. Cohen's summers are spent in Montreal. His most recent work **Death Of A Lady's Man** was published in 1978.*

As a student of Louis Dudek's, at McGill University in the fifties, Leonard Cohen thinks back thirty years to remember the class he attended, a class which contained several writers for "poets specially chose to study with Louis Dudek."

He remembers also those afternoons when the sun came pouring into the room in the Arts Building at McGill. To him Dudek was the ideal model of a teacher: a man of letters, and a poet; a measure of seriousness, and scholarship balanced with a friendly and helpful manner. "A sweet man, I never saw rancor in him; even his cynical moments were disinterested. One never felt he had an axe to grind. Dudek's style of teaching, his casualness appealed to me. He was always full of encouragement. He was generous with his time, and people who thought poetry was the most important thing gravitated to him. We sat at a long table with Dudek at the head. Frequently, lost in thought, he would lean so far back in his chair we thought he'd fall right over! He would either be reading Pound or discussing Yeats' spiritual system."

"I had started writing before I met him but it was he who published me first in *CIV/n* 4, a piece called "An Halloween Poem to Delight My Young Friends." When I was preparing my first book *Let us Compare Mythologies* Dudek suggested we form The McGill Poetry Series. My book was the first to be released in 1956. I went with Dudek to the Traymore Restaurant occasionally after class during the time he was putting together the series. The poem "Summer Night" in this book, refers to Dudek. We were in the country together with Aileen Collins. There was an amalgamation of our friends for a year or two. It was a time of talk and of evenings spent together."

"A lot of social gatherings of people who wrote took place during this period. We met often at F.R. Scott's place. Layton's place, or mine. Bob Currie was there and Phyllis Webb, among others. I spent many afternoons and evenings with Stephanie and Louis. I remember Stephanie, working on her Ph.D. in psychology, gave me the Rorschach test. She had us interested in the orgone accumulator box and Reichian theory."

"As a poet Dudek is smooth; he's even."

"I love the poem "Flower Song". "All I got out of you was a cactus,/ but even that, from you was okay." I love "Meditation Over A Wintry City". and "To An Unknown In A Restaurant". I admire the stately quiet music of his poetry in *Europe.*"

"His greatest contribution to Canadian writing is his sense of responsibility. Yes, Louis Dudek is a legend for me – and an important figure at a certain moment in my life. His example always is inspiring; his personal presence as a teacher and as a man. All his students love him."

March 10, 1982

Interview with Ron Everson

Everson has been publishing his poetry since the 1920's. He became acquainted with Dudek in the fifties when Contact Press published his first book A Lattice For Momos. Delta Canada, Dudek's later publishing venture with Gnarowski and Siebrasse, brought out three additional books of poetry by Everson. The two writers have kept in constant communication over the years. Everson's new selected poetry Everson at Eighty has been released by Oberon Press.

"Our relationship is really non-professional. If we're both in town we tend to have lunch about once a week together. Our main conversation is about how to start a renaissance or something like that. We do talk about poetry most of the time, but we are more friends than we are a couple of bards talking professionally."

Q. Do you feel you're the same kind of poet?

A: "Oh he's better than I am. He's more of a man of letters, and he knows several languages, so that he knows a great deal more than I do. He's worked himself up from the far east corner of Montreal, to a PhD from Columbia, to a full professorship at McGill, where he's been for thirty years. In the meantime he's started a few magazines, became a book publisher, and he's been influential in pushing ahead Canadian Poetry. As a critic he's first class — and fearless as well as objective. He was right in the 60's with his criticism. He hasn't been one to go out and make a lot of talk about himself. For example, he wouldn't advertise that he's been nominated for the Nobel Prize or some such thing. He is a genuinely modest man."

97

"Louis Dudek has spent nearly forty years trying to make Canadian poetry better; helping others enormously. He hasn't gone over into prose and he hasn't been involved in things other than poetry. He's also put up with being passed over. In fact he's received very little acclaim. He and Ralph Gustafson, it seems, are two poets who are excellent but who don't catch the public eye. Some people are just natural press agents for themselves — these two aren't. Fame often rests on some odd turn, but over the centuries it will rest on quality, It is not of first importance to Louis to be celebrated, however. He has the poetry in him and he writes."

Q: How do you feel Dudek's work has changed over the years?

A: "I think he's a little less positive than he used to be. When you read some of his early letters and pronouncements you realize that since then he's found out that there are many ways of writing poetry. That's happened to most of us. There was a time when to be modern was to get away from what was there before. Dudek's poetry has gotten better over the years ... more interesting ... he has an extremely active mind."

"I like his current poetry better than *Atlantis*, which was too much about standing around and looking at things in Naples, Rome, Paris, London. It seems he walked over all those cities and then commented on them. I don't know how one could do it differently, but he seemed to be ghosting around and peering at things, completely involved. In *Atlantis* he set out with a theme, and he was working on the theme all the time, so in a way *Europe* and *En Mexico* are better books than *Atlantis*, which could have been the great one. On the other hand *Poems from Atlantis* which came out recently has squeezed the best out of *Atlantis* and given it a clearer focus in my mind. Louis' poetry in *En Mexico* is very vivid and intense, similar to D.H. Lawrences' *Morning in Mexico*."

"For the last ten years or so his poetry has seemed to be about something of great significance. When we will get into a discussion of whether there is any purpose in the world, I am usually the agnostic and he is the religionist, and we do get to the point where there's a difference of opinion. He's more religious than I am — whatever religious means. He seems to think there is some purpose in life. Maybe his purpose is to go around hunting for what the purpose is. I simply can't understand anything about it. "

Q: How do you think he differs from other poets?

A: "Dudek comes close to being unique in Canada because he has never gone around with a crowd of other poets. The nearest he comes in recent years to having a close link with someone is with Ken Norris or Mike Gnarowski. He's been parts of various groups since way back in the forties, but the fact is that he has been a loner most of the time. He left The League of Canadian Poets, which has approximately 160 members, quite soon after it started because he thought they were including too many poets — he argued that there were probably only twenty good poets in the country. He isn't entirely unique in this, there are a few others that don't belong to the League. Layton is another."

"Being a loner Louis will disappear from time to time, and then a bit later I'll get hold of a paper he's presented somewhere or other that will explain his absence at that time. He works hard, you see. It's part of his modesty perhaps not to mention what he is busy with."

"He is different, though. I don't know other poets like him. He doesn't fall into any category. He's part of the Montreal group of poets, but he's quite different from any of them: in his content, in his way of doing things, his way of thinking, what he's done with his life all along, with Contact Press then Delta Magazine, then Delta Books, DC Press — always something new. He's a serious-minded man. He's more interested in writing poetry, in fact, and thinking about it, and writing about it, than he is in any acclaim he might gather."

"One thing that makes him different from others is that he doesn't mind taking an opposing view. In fact, he perhaps takes to it a little quicker than most people. Most people want an agreeable conversation, he prefers having a good argument. I think this whets his teeth and sharpens up his claws, it brightens his brain and certainly makes it hard for the other fellow — someone who has to put up a defence in support of something he just threw off carelessly! I know quite a few poets, but Dudek's by far the hardest to have a discussion with – with him you're immediately in deep ground and fighting for your life. Among the many poets that I know Dudek is the quickest on the draw, and superficially he will take up any argument on the spot. It's not necessarily serious. Simply a good mental exercise with him."

"Dudek has changed very little through the years. He has a fine consistent history that is of high quality and is different from most. He hasn't just gone on writing the next poem that comes into his head. He's had some plan about poems. Some poets just write until they have a book, while others artistically develop a theme and write about it. Louis' theme is his whole life. It's as though he's fortunate enough to see ahead, and to do this in spite of the difficulties of making a living and working in a college where poetry is I suppose the lowest form of life and where Canadians aren't in charge of most things in the department."

"Louis also has so many disciples. There are so many young poets that he's helped. This sets him apart. I don't know anybody who's helped younger poets as much as Dudek."

Everson then explains how he first met Dudek: "I contributed to some magazine he was editing or publishing. That's the usual way." In response to a question why they've remained friends over the years when friends drift apart and are so often lost Everson replies with a smile: "We have a bond. I love Louis Dudek and he tolerates me."

"Stephanie has told us that Louis is one of the world's greatest fathers. He used to spend three days a week with Gregory, his son, now getting his Ph.D in Toronto ... a brillant boy who has turned out very well. Dudek, by working along with Stephanie, has seen to giving Gregory a well-balanced upbringing. But Louis is not a boaster, so I didn't realize just how bright Gregory is until as recently as, say, four years ago, when he came to me during the summer selling vacuum cleaners. I thought he was just selling them to all his father's friends, but on questioning him I learned he has already sold twenty to people he didn't know

100

at all. This is in part a credit to Louis. In a broken home he still managed to cover all the bases and keep things going naturally for Gregory."

"Having a bitchy poet in a group (not to mention who) also has it's advantages not only for the poets, but for arousing public interest in poetry. Montreal has been far more successful at this than Toronto, for example. As well, Louis is an honest reviewer and critic. An honest critic is going to say what he thinks or he's got to quit being a critic."

"Louis and I are good friends. He's a decoration to Canadian literature, but much more than a decoration. He's been a serious integer and an important part of Canadian writing these last thirty or forty years. He has gone on all the time doing the thing he wants to do writing poetry — and being better at it than most of us."

13 July 1982
Montreal, Québec

Interview with Ralph Gustafson

This prominent Canadian writer has published eight volumes since 1935. He is responsible for the editions of **The Penguin Book of Canadian Verse** *that have been released regularly since the fifties. Born near Sherbrooke, Quebec, Gustafson studied at Oxford University, worked as a writer for some years in New York City, and returned finally to Canada, to North Hatley, to teach at Bishop's University. Now retired, his time is divided between his poetry and his music research.*

I've known Louis for a quarter of a century. From way back in New York when he was studying at Columbia University. I probably met him first through John Sutherland in Montreal in the 40's. That goes back to the famous little magazines of the forties: *First Statement* and the *Preview* group. At that time I was preparing *The Penguin Anthology of Canadian Literature*. No! ... I met Louis through Irving Layton. I was in New York and wrote to Layton telling him I'd like to print some of the younger Canadian poets, so Irving wrote a letter back to me and said "Sure, glad to be in your magazine" and drew my attention to a man who was writing good lyrics in Montreal, named Louis Dudek. (Now that was before Irving blew Louis sky-high on various matters.) So that's how I got to know Louis, at least by letter, and then I looked him up in Montreal frequently after that. So, I met John Sutherland through Louis. When Louis was in New York at Columbia with Stephanie, Ron Everson frequently came down and we had parties there and went to the opera, which was held in the old

Brewery House at the time. Then Louis used to come to our apartment on 168th Street with Irving, Frank Scott, Lekakis the sculptor, and others. So I knew him well in New York, and when I came up to teach at Bishop's, I'd see him at readings or meetings. At that time Louis was in close contact with Souster.

I think Louis has the best editorial mind in Canada. However, he apparently didn't care for *Conflicts In Spring*, my recent book, which he reviewed for the Toronto *Globe and Mail*.*

It's hard to chose amongst his books which I like the most. I think *Atlantis* impressed me very much because at that time I was getting interested in Ezra Pound, and you see Louis' style, after his first two or three books, changed – and probably Ezra Pound was the great influence. *Atlantis* impressed me because of what William Carlos Williams refers to as the broken style: the open line, and the variable line. It derives from William Carlos Williams, and Williams derives from Pound. 'Uncle Ez' is the father of us all.

There is one consistent line in Louis' poetry, and that's the intellectual line. It reigns through all his books; even through the different styles. Louis loves to meditate in verse. There's very little comedy, but there's a great deal of wit, which people tend to miss. *Epigrams* is full of wit; the irony is there too. So there is that consistency about Louis' work, even though the style changes. In his early work he started off with a conventional structure and form. He even used rhyme a great deal. Then suddenly there was this broken style deriving from the Williams and the Pound school, and I think he's still in it today. I feel it's unstructured, and too loose, so that Louis often loses his sense of formal rhythm. I don't mean he must write in iambic pentameter, but the line must be controlled, not sprawling. When this happens you lose the music. Now Louis is musical and plays the recorder with great panache, but sometimes his poems become verbally tone deaf.

---

* Dudek begs to differ. He has always been an admirer of Gustafson's poetry: see essay on Gustafson and Mandel in his *Selected Essays and Criticism*. "The review referred to dealt with ideas difficult to reconcile in Gustafson's poetry. The impression may have been more critical than it was meant to be. The occasional sniping comment is part of the program for healthy criticism."

Continuation 1 is Louis' style. It is consistent with him now and with his personality. He's learned his technique years ago. He's very pliant and his style is beautifully fitted to his own personality. But the danger I feel is that very often there's not enough architecture; not enough music. Now in saying that I may be defining my own poetry and wishing that Louis would write in my way. The ear is the criterion: the musical phrasing, not the visual appearance.

I always thoroughly, deeply enjoyed being in contact with him, and talking not only on the technique of poetry but more to simply exchange minds, and Louis' greatest love is to argue. He will even demolish a stable position in order to get the argument going. So it's fun, and we've talked philosophy and God, as everybody does, but with Louis it's always cogent. He's a very erudite fellow. We started in New York. I remember talking to him about Plato, and how Plato was bats because he wasn't concrete (you can't be a poet without being concrete); and then about god in Ways Mills ... and I don't know what else. Many subjects! Louis once lost a glove and we went for a walk into the bush to try and find it; and of course we talked as we walked, and as we did this we found God — as well as the glove!

Isn't it interesting ... having discussed God with Louis, I still don't know whether he's a Catholic, a Brahmin, a Zen-ist. How nice it is to know that I still don't know. So that's fine. We're free of all the paraphanalia of institutionalized religion.

Another thing about Louis which left a historical mark in Canadian writing is his magazine *Delta*. It ran for nine years. I contributed some of my poetry to it. At that time it was avant garde, in the sense that it was original. He was presenting Ezra Pound years ago. I was in Venice in April, 1982, and had a wonderful afternoon with Olga Rudge, Pound's mistress. We talked about Uncle Ez all afternoon and she said to me, knowing that I was a poet from Canada: "Do you happen to know a fellow named Louis Dudek?" And so I went to town on the magazine *Delta* and on *DK/Some Letters of Ezra Pound*. I go to all the Pound conferences, in Maine, London, and so on. They usually mention Louis for having put out that book of letters, which is wonderful.

My impressions of Louis have never changed over the years so far as our friendship is concerned. These discussions we'd have, and bull sessions on Plato, and music, and what not, continue, and I also follow Louis in his criticism. His stance is my stance usually. So I'm a great admirer, not because he agrees with me but because he puts his finger right on the point of what a book is trying to do, and whether the book succeeds or not. Once you read Louis you know. He's one of the few good critics we have in Canada. Generally the newspaper critics are deplorable in Canada, but whenever Louis appears in *The Gazette* and *The Globe and Mail* as well as the magazines, he's always worth reading.

In a quarter of a century our relationship has changed little — we've grown closer, that's all. I only have one beef with Louis, and that is that my Penguin Anthology, which was the first to break down the colonial approach to Canadian poetry, was never mentioned by Louis or Mike Gnarowski in *The Making of Modern Poetry in Canada*. (Sixty thousand copies were printed in the first edition in England, and it isn't even mentioned in their book!) *

The most unique thing about Louis is his intellectual capacity. It runs right through everything. You can't read him without being engaged intellectually. That doesn't mean you read everything and are moved by everything he's written, because very often the emotion isn't there in conjunction with the meaning — but there's always the meaning whether the form is right or not. It's bound to be interesting, valuable and original. So when Dudek meditates in verse: listen! It's something good!

14 July 1982
North Hatley, Québec

---

* Dudek apologizes. "It has always been meant to be included in the revised edition, but this has somehow been endlessly delayed."

Interview with D. G. Jones

Poet, professor of literature at the University of Sherbrooke, D.G. Jones is the author of **Butterfly on Rock** *a highly admired book of Canadian criticism. As a young poet, Jones attended Dudek's very first classes in Modern Poetry at McGill in the fifties, and later while at Queens he maintained his contacts with the Montreal scene. He has taught at Guelph and at Bishop's University.* **The Sun is Axeman** *(1961) was awarded the Governor General's award for poetry. Though Jones and Dudek hold different views concerning myth and reality in Canadian writing, there is a grudging mutual respect apparent when either discusses the other's work.*

"I got to know Louis Dudek the last year I was at McGill. He had just returned from New York and the head of the department at McGill wanted to get him in the department, but there was no way he could be given a full course. So he was given a part-time night course. My wife rounded up a dozen of us and he had a course. We took it as an extra course and paid for it. They wanted to keep him there so they could hire him full time the next year, partly because Patrick Anderson had disappeared in the Far East and never came back. Professor Files, who was head of the department at that time, knew Louis and wanted to get him on staff. I expect now Dudek is a lot more academic as a teacher than he was then during his first course. He had us reading modern American poetry and he communicated a certain enthusiasm for this quite obviously. In fact it was fairly influential in a way, because I started reading a few of Pound's *Cantos* and proposed it as a thesis topic for my M.A., which was accepted, even though I hadn't at that moment read more than three or four of the *Cantos.*"

"Louis emphasized the sense of the spoken voice in the poetry. I remember him reading, and getting us to read the poems. His enthusiasm for the poetry and the form was communicated. In the course of that year, through Louis, I met Irving Layton. I started to write poems and I showed them to Louis; he was much more enthusiastic about them than Patrick Anderson had been. Louis was interested in getting young people to write, and that continued for a number of years. He was a kind of contact between generations and I think he saw it as a role for him to play at this time. When I left for Queen's Louis kept in touch and continued to stimulate me to write; he also accepted one or two of my poems for *CIV/n* during that period."

"It was partly because of that course and that meeting that at the end of my M.A. year at Queen's my wife decided that several people at Queen's and Louis and Irving should all get together up at our cottage in Ontario for a party. So we had a long weekend in which Louis and Irving turned up and John Harney, who is now in politics rather than poetry, and rather unexpectedly, and late, Frank Scott and A.J.M. Smith, whom I met for the first time. So we had quite a session. It was then that Frank proposed, late one night, the Kingston Writers' Conference; getting money from the Guggenheim Foundation for it. This conference was held in Kingston a year or two later, that was, in the fifties. That was one way to get to know a number of Canadian poets personally. The relationship between Louis and Frank and A.J.M. Smith continued over the years. So it was a very influential kind of meeting and it gave you a sense of being in contact with the major poets at that time."

"Scott and Smith and Louis and Irving were the mature poets who were active and influential then, along with Raymond Souster, whom I didn't meet till later. But it was Irving, Louis and Souster who thought up the idea of the community Press – a co-operative press: Contact Press. And it was with that press that I got my first book published. So outside the university magazine my first poems were published in Souster's *Contact* and Louis' *CIV/n*. And my first book was published with Contact, and that was the result of these 'contacts' that first began with Louis.''

"Working in the context of your own literature with these people, partly, had to do with Louis Dudek because he turned his students onto poetry. I then followed my interest in French and English Canadian poetry when I came to Sherbrooke.''

"In the 60's the people in Vancouver started to write under the influence of Creeley, Olson and the Black Mountain poets. Louis became annoyed and highly critical of them in his review articles. This looked like a rather strange thing for Louis to be doing. He seemed very reactionary and conservative at that point in time, because in a way many of the things he had been emphasizing as models and influences in Pound and in Williams were directly related to that influence of Olson. There's always been a split in that respect in Louis' own work; it's a little puzzling, and I suspect it undermines to a certain degree the impact he's had in poetry and the effect of his own writing.''

"When I wrote *Butterfly On Rock* Louis told me: "This is crazy. This is poetry; it's not criticism.'' He had no great use for Frye and he was busy writing articles in effect against certain other influences that had developed in English Canadian poetry. He developed a case against what he called the myth-makers: Frye's influence on Jay Macpherson and James Reaney. I think he more or less developed this term as well as the quarrel between what he called the myth-makers and the social realists. He argued from the point of view of social realism in poetry and criticized the so-called myth-makers, who were inclined to use large imaginative forms. I mean myths, either classic myths or any sort of imagery on a mythical level. Louis had a tremendous resistance towards that. On the one hand he tends to be a kind of realist; on the other hand, the whole point about poems like *Atlantis* is that they turn on the image of an ideal city. There is, essentially, a myth behind that, an ideal city which is sunk and which has to be raised out of the depths of the sea, whether you describe that as rising from the

109

inarticulate and unconscious to the conscious and articulate, to culture, or whether you just call it the inchoate and undeveloped as related to the whole civilizing process. For example, it's the word which he takes from Pound and gives as the title to the magazine *CIV/n* civilization: *CIV/n: not a one man job.* This is essentially a large mythical pattern. Yet he's very loath to recognize this and deal with it in a straightforward fashion. You have the impression that he has to ground anything that tends towards such a large and ideal mythical design in a kind of journalistic realistic detail, as for example so many of his poems gather up bits and pieces of scenery in travelling in Mexico and Europe. What he hears on the street, what he sees written on the walls, in the newspapers, what people see on the beach. It's a kind of realistic gathering up of general details. He tries to make, I suppose, his mythical design implicit in that realistic detail and have it emerge out of it. It's a rather large and somewhat laborious process to make that happen. On the other hand he has poems that almost abstract. For example, when he talks about the nature of reality as being a constant collision of particles and energies out of which comes the shaping of various individual forms, that is almost an abstract poetry.''

"He runs from the little aphorisms and maxims and witty epigrams to this long kind of poem ... he runs from a kind of 17th Century squib fire-cracker, or 18th Century wit poetry to a kind of imagistic poem, and so he gets himself a little all over the map. Often, he seems to be on two sides at once, and this has always been confusing to me reading his poetry, poem to poem. It reflects a kind of conflict within the poetry and within the personality of Dudek himself. It is difficult to focus the image you have of Louis' vision, if you take the work as a whole.''

Q: You want to bring it down to just one vision?

A: "Well all this makes the man look a little inconsistent or uncertain; and he jumps around a little bit in his critical procedures too. You never can be quite sure at any moment when he will go from being avant garde to reactionary. Sometimes this is a result I suppose of certain emotions, as it is a result of intellectual convictions. Sometimes a combination of both. He can lambaste modern art at certain times, and yet he is associated with the movement that represents certain kinds of modern art in Canada; so it looks a little odd.''

''My main reservation critically is that he's too much an English Canadian poet. He's rather close to the mainstream of English poetry, and that is quite different from French Canadian poetry, and is very close to certain American poets – which is precisely why we borrowed from them so well, and so easily, and so willingly.''

''The English Canadian poet, I suspect, tends as a rule to be realistic, tends to stick to the representational and the representative; he tries to get a representative image of the world; he is concerned above all with space – that is, he's really horizontal in his vision. He's right down to earth.''

''It was Louis Dudek who, in fact, made one of the most simple distinctions between English Canadian and French Canadian poetry, stated somewhat negatively: ''The trouble with French Canadian poets is they never get their feet on the ground. The trouble with English Canadian poets is they hardly ever get their feet off the ground.'' They're pedestrian. They stick to the ground and they are obsessed with space. The articulation of space. The organization of space. How one relates to space: whether it's going to be a kind of pastoral relationship or a kind of imperial relationship. The poetry is full of images of roads, whether they're rivers or highways, or airways and the whole problem of transportation and communication is absolutely central. The elaboration of an order, a spatial order, a civilized order, a civic world, a civic space, is an essential preoccupation of English Canadian poetry from Goldsmith at the beginning of the 19th Century to Kirby, Crawford, E.J. Pratt, Earle Birney, and Dennis Lee. The whole bias of the imagination with a physical world, a material world, a special world, a realistic world and a realistic mold and a real suspicion of anything that is visionary, that is imaginative, that moves too quickly into the worlds of allegory, symbol, surrealism, myth is something most English Canadians are wary of. They approach it very gingerly. They like to anchor everything in reality

111

first of all, and as Dorothy Livesay said, the documentary poem is the privileged Canadian genre, just as the documentary film is, in English Canada."

"Louis in a sense is writing a kind of documentary poem. He may have a vision of *Atlantis* but he's got it rooted in time and space with very particular details. The point about *Atlantis* is that it's a vertical vision. It's basically a myth. There is a whole ideal world that he wants to talk about, which we should realize, but he talks about it in a typically English Canadian fashion."

"I have a deliberate reaction to this, partly in reaction to myself and my own English Canadianism. I'm really interested in this other kind of poetry. Part of my poetry, I know, is anchored often very firmly in a particular space. And it moves, only after being so anchored, out into some more speculative, slightly more unrealistic phase."

"In many of the early poems in my first book or so, I suppose I was learning very rapidly or working fairly closely with some of the kinds of things that Louis was doing. So yes, it can be said that there is an affinity of sorts between us. Louis was doing Pound and Williams. So the interest in imagism, and the sharp image and so on, is very central for me, and my whole imagination is quite pictorial, visual, graphic, and associated with this kind of image. All that comes through partly with the reinforcement of the American poets, and Louis' presence and teaching, and what he stood for at that time. That affinity remains and remains very strong. It's all part of what's happened since Louis and Irving and Souster came on the Canadian poetry scene. For one thing, with these poets the major influence from outside Canada shifted from England to the United States – they shifted it, most powerfully. Dudek, Layton and Souster made Imagism, brought in by Pound, explicit, and in fact they established contacts, literally, in the magazine *Contact*, with later American poets. It made these poets visible to a small group of people here; it told them this is the influence to follow."

"Well the influence of concrete images in Williams and Olson, with their emphasis on geography, on local space, on language and culture as related to your own personal and community space – all this in a sense goes with the general bias, it seems to me, of English Canadian poetry, and of English Canadian culture, which is one of the reasons why this American influence comes in. It's very strong and very central."

"Yes, Dudek and I are alike in some ways. It is true that we share the imagistic interest of picking up particular details of one's world. There's also a larger concern, which manifests itself in part as a concern for our society, for civilization, but also tends to become metaphysical in the end. I think Louis and I share all that, along with, perhaps, in varying degrees, other Canadians."

"We differs also, however, because first of all I don't write quite as long poems as Louis. I don't keep notebooks and I don't make either travelogues or that kind of large-scale documentary poems. Critically my bias is to encourage the larger imaginative patterns. this is where we begin to differ, in our sympathy towards certain modes and certain attitudes – well, we've twitted each other about these differences but we simply maintain them."

"In short, I would say really that Louis lacks, like many English writers, the courage of his convictions as an imaginative man or as a writer, the conviction that imaginative patterns are significant, powerful and don't always have to be backed up by some journalist, as it were, who comes along and gathers up all the little details."

Q: So you are criticizing, in part, the fact that his touchstone is reality?

A: "Yes, because I don't believe in that. What one calls reality is usually a construct. I believe that in a very powerful way the reality in which one lives is culturally defined. It is, in effect, a myth. When I say it's a myth I don't mean that it's unreal. I don't mean it's a diversion, I don't mean it's a disease or anything like that. Your reality is something you happen to inherit to a certain degree with your culture. It is what you call reality, and it is a myth, so far as it is articulate, and so far as it leads you to look one way rather than another, The difference between English Canada

113

and French Canada is that to a large extent they live inside different realities.''

Q: Do you say you are writing from within the French Canadian point of view, while Dudek is writing inside the English Canadian view of reality?

A: "Neither of these realities is static. Neither is perfect either. In fact, the whole dynamism on both sides is to try and change them, especially because both have become (and that was more obvious in French) painfully unacceptable as a reality. They've tried to change their whole reality. the French Canadian writers knew, in a sense, that if you wanted to change the reality all you had to do was change the text. Louis perhaps wouldn't accept that statement. He'd say 'That's bullshit' or something of the sort." (Jones chuckles) "Louis in his extreme bias is a Dr. Johnson. When he's pushed up to the wall he kicks a stone and says 'That's reality!'''

"He favors Raymond Souster, and he emphasizes this realistic side in his own poetry and in the poetry of other people, and he uses that phrase − social realism − as if he himself was a hard-headed serious fellow, whereas these other myth-makers are doubtful characters. But the myth-makers, as far as I'm concerned, especially when you get into Gwen MacEwen or Robert Kroetsch, come at it more deeply from the point of view of modern criticism and structuralism. What they realize is that they transform the modes of seeing and the modes of expression, and that is more important than transforming the matter, because it's the mode itself that actually determines in many ways what you see. It determines your reality, and that is as real as anything. The problem I see in much of English Canadian poetry, in other words, is a certain lack of conviction in the imagination itself, in the forms of the imagination.''

Q: Is that why you didn't discuss Dudek in your book *Butterfly on Rock?*

A: "Partly, I suppose. Well, he does get in, I believe in a quotation or two. But I was working with certain themes, and cer-

114

tain patterns of imagery. I could have got him in there, in a few places, but in a way it would have been rather laborious. I could have used hunks of *Atlantis*, but then the amount of space it would take to make up 'significant detail' would have been somewhat inefficient and repetitious, since I already had that. I could have made certain points, as I recall — it's a long time ago — but I do recall thinking of taking up a number of Louis' poems, but then thinking that it was getting to be too much — it was swelling my chapter up and it was taking a long time to get it out, to illustrate it properly. I finally took out what I did have, except for one or two quotations, because it made the chapter unwieldy and it didn't seem necessary. At this point, as well, Louis was not one of the most widely read poets. But it was a question partly of the size of the thing.''

"There were things that I had to say that I could have pointed to in his work as an example, but it became in a sense unwieldy, and that was one of the main reasons. I would have liked to put more in, and I think I did at one point, but I took it out for that reason.''

"When I was at Queens, and four to five years after that, when Contact Press was running, Louis was very present. With the Magazines *CIV/n*, then Delta, he was writing me and all kinds of people across the country and he was always saying how we had to have more new poets. He was full of enthusisam. But after a while he split with Layton, he was getting less frequent replies from the other people. The poetry scene seemed to have moved from Montreal to Toronto, and then of course to Vancouver. At this point I think he got somewhat depressed, and he withdrew, so he was not felt as a visible presence. At that point, when I started writing that book, I had no particular idea of any major difference in outlook between Louis and myself. Well, perhaps I realize he had those reservations about Northrop Frye, which I didn't share. That's true of other people that I know. But it was after the book came out that I could feel most distinctly a difference of bias between myself and Louis.''

Q: Does this have to divide and separate the two of you?

A: "Oh no, I'm good friends with Louis. If Louis has reasons for believing and writing his way he can go ahead and do it – as I do, my way and my own thing. I like Louis very much as a person, and he's been in a much better mood the last number of years, and its been great to see him this way. Yes, the recognition he's received in the last few years – well, that makes everybody feel better as a rule."

Q: As a critic, where would you place Louis Dudek today in the scheme of things?

A: "Well I think he's been the bridge between generations. He was a contact between generations – between American and Canadian poetry. He helped to bring in some very striking influences from the United States, and to shift the pattern of influence from British to American. He helped to make our poetry a little sharper and clearer. He does continue, in his practice as a poet and as a critic, an essentially English kind of concern, both in terms of style or poetics and in terms of theme. He is in a sense what I would consider in the mainstream or the main tradition of English Canadian poetry. He has been of major importance in representing that point of view in publishing; he's been quite catholic at times in his magazines. His magazines tended to bring out that point of view, and they represented that point of view in poetry, so this was of major importance. It also disturbs me or irritates me at times, because it seems to perpetuate a suspicion of the imagination and to continue the pedestrian side of English Canadian writing, both English Canadian Literature and English Canadian culture. It seems to me he differs, oddly enough, and quite strikingly, from the early Irving Layton. It's very paradoxical that Layton should end up with Louis Dudek, criticizing Frye; in some ways Layton is closer, far closer than Louis, to those people who have an imaginative daring, are willing to use symbols and myths without immediate reference to local situations, to particular historical reality. It seems to me, from A.M. Klein, with his Jewish background, and A.J.M. Smith with his Christian background, and right down from Klein through Layton to Cohen, the line goes in a sense to Northrop Frye and to Jay Macpherson and Reaney and MacEwen and so on. Dudek, apart from

116

what he brings in from outside, is more in line with the new Canadian poets, through the long poem in the 19th Century."

Q: Would you also say there is a line from Pound to Dudek to D.G. Jones, or would we put you under Frye only?

A: "Well, I'm sort of in between the two. Basically I'm an English Canadian poet. But there are certain elements that have always fascinated me in French Literature; Mallarmé and certain French Canadian poets have fascinated me."

Q: I don't see Dudek as insular inside of English Canada. He's always championed cooperation between English and French writers in Canada.

A: "I don't see him as insular. I just say that he works within that tradition. He's anything but insular; in a sense, one of the chief things he's done is bring influences in from the outside. In the long poem, what he did was to bring Pound's mosaic approach to the long poem, which up to that time had basically been mainly narrative discursive. The basic model was a mixture of Goldsmith and Burns. Goldsmith's "Deserted Village" is one of the archetypal poems of English Canadian Literature, which I see Dennis Lee, in "Civil Elegies", rewriting two hundred years later. It tends to be descriptive, discursive, narrative, as a basic poem, and it tends to be very linear. The narrative may turn into a mere itinerary, as in a Kirby poem, where he goes up the St. Lawrence and the poem becomes a long itinerary of places. The same is true of Sangster's: "St. Lawrence and the Saguenay". It is either that or narrative, as in most of Pratt's poems, they all have a linear narrative structure, and this is what Louis changed when he brought Pound in. He writes a long poem but without the linear narrative structure.

Q: What do you think is Dudek's best work?

A: "I like certain of the short lyrics and I like parts of *Europe, En Mexico* and *Atlantis*. What I also like and think fun are his squibs, sayings, maxims and epigrams, but what I'm interested myself in is a different kind of poetry of vision. I think he moves towards that in the longer poems. Something like *Atlantis* is

117

certainly the most ambitious and probably the most important work, though I haven't really sat down to digest it carefully and in detail, to form an absolute opinion of it."

Q: If someone said to you "That is what you should know about Dudek." What would that be?

A: "One of the things I would say about Dudek, and not always about other writers, is that I think of him as a person before I think of him as a writer – a friend, a teacher. He is a serious-comic character of extreme generosity who always makes me feel good when I see him, even if he is irritating in some of the things that he says or does – I always feel good, and I like him basically more, despite whatever may be irritating in what he does. I mean he can read a poem three lines long and give a half an hour's talk on it. He's an inveterate teacher. He cannot stop teaching."

Q: So you are the critic who has started the rumor that he's didactic and rhetorical?

A: "Well, Louis will teach you what he's found out about particle physics in the middle of a birthday party!"

Q: What else do you know about him that sets him apart from the others?

A: "In conclusion? It would have been quite a different world without him. Of yes, he has definitely changed my world ..."

14 July 1982
North Hatley, Quebec

118

Interview with Ken Norris

For his PhD at McGill University, Norris worked under Louis Dudek on a history of the literary magazines in Canada. A founding member of Véhicule Press, and one of the socalled "Véhicule Poets", Norris has been one of the prime movers in the resurgence of English language poetry in Montreal since the 70's. In this period he has helped edit and publish more than fifty books by other poets and under his own signature, with various small press imprints.

"Yes, I would have to say that working with Louis Dudek and getting to know him has had a considerable effect upon me. In *The Book of Fall* I wrote about having a dream in which I was Dudek's adopted son, and it is true that I sometimes feel that way. I grew up in a working class family, with a Catholic up-bringing, just as he did. My parents weren't highly educated, they hadn't gone beyond high school, so it's been important for me to know someone who has had a similar background and yet has obviously transcended the bounds of his class through education and a commitment to the world of ideas. It's given me perspective on how I can lead my own life.

"Ezra Pound once told Louis "to become a solid man" and I think that this was a piece of advice he really took to heart. He passed on this same advice to me a few years ago; I think I've taken it less to heart, but maybe that's because there's less need for

119

that now. One can live out the life of art in the 1980's more easily than in the 1950's. That's due in part to the creative atmosphere that Louis and others like him have made possible.

"I first met Louis in 1975 when I came to McGill to begin my doctorate. I soon decided that I would study with him. One of the reasons was that I felt he was a bridge to the early Moderns. I knew about his correspondence with Pound and figured I could get a good Imagist/Vorticist education through him.

"I had also become aware of his work, having read the *Collected Poetry* the previous summer. I was impressed by the quality and volume of poetry there and I couldn't understand why his reputation in Canada wasn't much greater than it was. This sense of an injustice was increased, I suppose by my reading some of Layton's poetry and not finding much in it. I had been in Montreal from 1974 to 1977 and I had arrived back in Montreal from the States in February of 1975, I had published my first book *Vegetables*, and had begun to pick up on Canadian mythology. I knew about the Layton-Dudek controversy but I couldn't understand why Layton was so famous and Dudek wasn't. In fact, it seemed to me that the literary establishment had made a grave error: it had spotlighted the wrong man. Only with time did I come to understand how conservative a literary traditon held its ground in Canada and how Dudek's revolutionary poetic went against the grain of practically all the aspects of that tradition.

"Of course, when I first met him even Dudek seemed incredibly conservative to me. My *Vegetables* book had preceded me, Louis had read it before I arrived, and I felt he didn't like it very much. To him it was just another book of "pop art." It took me quite a while to begin to understand his antagonism toward popular culture, because I had been steeped in it: comic books, television, rock and roll, the whole works. And it took Louis a while to become adjusted to the poetics of the Véhicule poets, a group of which I was a card-carrying member. In the mid-seventies he had stopped being a "scenemaker". DC Books were gearing down, and Véhicule Press was just starting up. Gradually he began to be interested in what we were doing.

"As far as my education at McGill was concerned, there weren't any formal classes to attend; I was working under the project system. Occasionally I'd sit in on Louis' graduate seminar on Modernism, but mostly I'd go and sit with him in his office for an hour or so on Tuesday mornings while the school year was on. Theoretically we were talking about my project on Canadian little magazines, but we usually spent about five minutes talking about that and the rest of the time on different aspects of Western literature and all branches of the humanities. And of course I would occasionally pump him for information on how *First Statement* was run or what had happened with Contact Press at such and such a time; and then I'd go out and institute similar policies with *Cross-Country* (a magazine I was running) or with Véhicule Press. After a long talk about the *First Statement/Preview* conflict of the forties I went off and wrote an article that tried to provoke a similar conflict between New Delta and Véhicule Press. We wanted the same kind of energy.

"In the past few years I think Louis has turned to poetry again more fully. One reason, I think, is that he has finally been able to identify his true poetic heirs. I think he felt antagonized and offended by a lot of the anti-poetic and subversive activity of the 1960's. Those times upset him — seeing young poets turn to anarchy, drugs, trying to undermine what he values very much: the university and its tradition of knowledge. I think he supported many of that generation's goals, but not their methods. This alienated him from the literary avant-garde, of which he is really the founding father in Canada. Recently I think he's started to realize that presses like Coach House and Véhicule, as it was in the seventies, represent an extension of his own publishing work. He asked in the 1950's "Où sont les jeunes" and the poets he called for only started making their appearance in the late sixties and early seventies. Now he can see the relationship between, say, bp Nichol's *the martyrology* and his own *Atlantis*.

"Also, it's obvious that there's a Dudek revival of sorts afoot. I think he is going to enjoy a resurrection similar to that of William Carlos Williams. It's only now that a new generation of writers is coming along and acknowledging the importance of his

121

achievement and his energy. Suddenly there are a number of people all realizing in different ways that Dudek had the guts to write a new kind of poetry in Canada when no one else was doing it. Louis has been a truly pioneering writer. His non-narrative long poems broke new ground. *Europe, En Mexico,* and *Atlantis* are important touchstones for those of us writing now.

"Louis' reputation as an inspiring teacher and as an important scenemaker cannot be disputed. He's created an entire environment for poetry to exist where once there was only a vacuum. Frank Davey has said in *From There To Here* that no other poet has been as important to succeding generations of Canadian poets, and I agree with that verdict. Dudek has always been leading us into the future with his poetry. He's also instilled in many of us a sense of cultural responsibility.

"Personally, the greatest impression of Dudek's poetry for me has come from the sea meditations: *Europe* 16 and 95, the epilogue from *Atlantis*, "Coming Suddenly to the Sea," "The Sea at Monhegan." That, to me, is poetry in possession of an incredible mystical power. For all the ideas and rationality in his work, I still find his strength to be poems that deal with emotions and religious feeling. There is a contradiction in his work between the heart and the intellect. I suppose that's why I find the sea poetry so powerful: we see the ordering mind there considering what seems to be chaotic yet is creative and remains as the source of all life."

7 June 1982
Montreal, Quebec

122

Interview with Frank R. Scott

One of Canada's first modern poets, F.R. Scott, son of Archdeacon Frederick George Scott, was born in Quebec City. He was schooled there until he studied law at Bishop's University before attending Oxford as a Rhodes Scholar. His first poems were published in 1925, and as recently as 1983, he confesses that he still has poetry rumbling around in his brain. A brilliant man, an activist, a wit, and a scholar, Scott has always contributed his time and energy to Canadian politics, law, and literature. He collaborated with A.J.M. Smith to found the **McGill Fortnightly Review** *then the* **Canadian Mercury,** *as well as the book* **New Provinces.** *He shared in the founding of* **Preview,** *a magazine which merged in 1945 with* **First Statement** *to form* **Northern Review.** *It was in the* **Preview** *years that he first met the young poet Louis Dudek. Their relationship has spanned the years and increased in warmth while many changes have been wrought on the Montreal poetry scene. Scott has received two Governor General awards, one for* **Essays on the Constitution;** *the other in 1982 for his* **Collected Poetry.** *He is the recipient of the Therese Casgrain Award for 1983.*

"I've known Louis many years", says Frank Scott. "He has gradually assumed the position of a close friend and he's remained close ever since – the best friend we have in Montreal. He's a perfect friend for me because he is a warm and generous human being; he knows poets and poetry, and he has good ideas about them. What I like about his ideas is that he is not afraid to swim against the current and criticize the younger poets for their sloppiness, though this has earned him a lot of criticism on their part. He's not afraid to speak up and state his opinion."

Louis Dudek, Scott says, is "a different type of poet from Souster or Layton." Scott quietly adds that Irving Layton has been rather vicious at times, not just to Louis but to other writers also, Ron Everson for example. Scott feels that Layton's vindictive letters have in part prevented Dudek from achieving the recognition he deserved.

"What I like about Louis is his philosophical bent," Scott goes on. "He wants to get into the real critical meaning of poetry and work it out. He's very quick to pick up a new idea of a philosophical type. We could be having a talk, when suddenly a statement will set him off and he'll want to discuss it at considerable length. It makes him a lively conversationalist. I don't always agree with him, and I don't think he himself always agrees with his own experimental statements. He works it out as he goes along. He's a very lively person ... a great asset."

Scott adds that Louis Dudek is a well-rounded individual. A good father; a good chess player — he's now trying to beat the computor! And — a person to whom music is very important in his life. Smiling, Scott recalls how, after hearing a tape of himself playing the violin, Dudek took up the mandolin: "He's rather charming with the mandolin. He plays it gently." At Frank's 80th birthday party held in North Hatley at their country home, "Louis was there and Ron Sutherland. Ron played the bagpipes. You never heard a more curious combination. Sutherland marched up and down the balcony of our country home while Louis sat and strummed on the mandolin."

The Scotts also remember the Sunday afternoon they were to meet Louis Dudek and Aileen Collins at the Dudek's country home in Way's Mills. the Scotts arrived but there was no one there. Returning home — a distance of fifteen miles — rather puzzled, they rounded the corner of the house to find the Dudek's waiting patiently on the verandah. They had all got their wires crossed!

"I've one more thing to say about Louis which has struck me," F.R. Scott says. "I know that his teaching courses on Canadian Literature have been very much appreciated by young students who went through Arts at McGill and then came into Law. The ones that have been touched by the hand of Dudek have a little more imagination and are somehow different. One person – he shall be nameless – gave up the practice of law and went to work in the cultural life of Canada. Some others have done the same thing. I had the impression from them that it was an unforgettable experience to have been taught by Louis Dudek, even on a subject not so easily made into magic as Canadian Poetry. He awoke something in his students which changed their lives, if they had the real creative imagination, and many of them do have. So this has been a real contribution to McGill, having that going on in the English Department.''

''He has also been very generous looking after younger poets and getting them published, and of course in running his own publications. He's been a real help to poets – to John Asfour, the Lebanese blind poet – to Jagdip Maraj the Caribean poet – as well as others who've come up here. He is the chemical equation that makes things happen, a catalyst.

''Louis has a wonderful sense of humour and has written a lot of light verse, epigrams, brief statements. One of my favorites is the epigram:

''Of all sad fates the avant gardes' the worst –
They were going nowhere, and they got there first.''

Scott laughs warmly, adding that he's always fancied himself as a bit of an avant gardist. When I ask Scott if he considers Dudek avant garde he replies: ''Not particularly. He's not very impressed by people always trying to get up something new when all they're doing is changing things around and not getting the fundamental new image. I like that side of Louis Dudek. Of course, some of the things he puts down are rather trivial – though he would be quite happy and amused to say so himself – there's a kind of joyousness in this. Avant Garde? Well, I wouldn't want to make that the label.''

When asked where Dudek stands in the context of other Canadian writers Scott replies thoughtfully, ''The word Canadian writers covers such a multitude of sins and so few virtues. He certainly stands way above most of them. I think that he's had a note of sanity in his criticism about the seriousness of poetry that you can't be casual on regardless of form or principles. I don't feel Louis has quite had the recognition he merits but that seems to be changing. Frank Davey's recent criticism of him is good and gives him the recognition he rightfully deserves.''

F.R. Scott
12 May 1982

Interview with Raymond Souster

Souster is well known as 'the poet of Toronto'. He has been associated with Louis Dudek since the early years when the little magazine First Statement was being produced by John Sutherland. With Dudek, and poet Irving Layton, Souster started Contact Press in the early fifties. In 1968, he was one of the founding members and Chairman of The League of Canadian Poets. Four volumes of his "Collected Poetry" have been published by Oberon Press; a fifth is to be released soon.

"One thing readers would want to know about Louis Dudek," Raymond Souster says, "is the influence of Ezra Pound in his poetry. That is: it was central in his work around the time *Europe* was written – not now. However, I think there always will remain some of that spirit of Pound in him. For example: he still feels as Pound felt that there are certain ideals worth fighting for, that the press muzzles the writer, that there is something there to attack ... that there is a press and a money establishment that runs things."

"Louis is essentially a lyric poet," Souster goes on. "You wouldn't say he's a nationalistic Canadian though. He's more of a universal poet for he addresses the universal – you could even see him easily as part of the American line of writers. In this respect, he is an individual Canadian poet, unique in that no one has written quite like him – no one has exactly followed his example, in content, just as no one has followed mine."

"When Louis published *East Of The City* with Ryerson, I published *Go to Sleep World* at the same time. But mine was the last book in that Ryerson series, they found it wasn't economically feasible to bring out any more. Ryerson then switched to chapbooks. Irving Layton couldn't get published anywhere either so the three of us were in the same boat. That's pretty well when Contact Press was born, we had to find another means to publish our work. We started with *Cerberus* and went on from there."

According to Souster, "*Cerberus* is the book that led people to link us together and maybe assume things that weren't really true about us — that we were close-knit. We were just three people together, who were finding it hard to publish and found it convenient to publish in a book together. I think if you read our little prefaces to *Cerberus* you will see we all had quite different ideas about poetry."

"I think *Europe* is Dudek's single strongest work," Souster continues. "But some of his nicest lyrics are in his first volume *East Of The City*. My criticism of *Atlantis* is that he's retelling some of the same material from *Europe*."

Regarding their personal friendship he comments: "We never spent time together." He explains further: "We haven't seen each other very much over the years, really. With my wife's health we haven't been to Montreal in ten years. We used to go every year." The myth linking Dudek, Layton and Souster, according to Souster, is really just that — a myth. "I've only seen Layton once in the last twelve years, and the last several times I've seen Dudek we've been very stiff with each other. We've corresponded over the years but we've never confided in each other. Our common bonds are in the past but I have good thoughts and feelings about him. We've both tried to keep our integrity as poets. Our personality wouldn't have allowed us to be on Jack McClelland's bandwagon. We're not into promoting our own work. That's not for us, to talk up the book. I feel that if the poetry has any worth it may take longer to get through to people, but the people that want to read it, eventually will read it. This is what Dudek and I have in common."

128

Remembering the 1940's he says, "The First Statement people were influenced by Americans. The Preview people were still influenced by Auden and that school, so there was quite a difference in our literary preferences. Louis' writing had a fairly clean American line which we'd identify with William Carlos Williams. Louis gave me Williams' book later, in 1951, I hadn't encountered Williams in any real way till then. It was at the same meeting that Louis brought me two copies of Cid Corman's *Origin*. He didn't think too much of *Origin*. At the time I accepted his judgment of *Origin*, but a year later I changed my mind, that is, after re-reading those issues, and so got in touch with Corman. Louis wasn't much interested in Corman or Creeley. Pound was Louis' God. I'm talking about the 40's. He's quite different now."

Souster adds to this: "Louis is a person who has had his own definite opinions and he is not very flexible once he has made up his mind. He has very closely defined ideas about literature. He sometimes thought young people were publishing too early, and too much. That was a constant refrain, in the sixties; but then if he found someone that he thought had talent he was the first to bring out their book."

Souster holds that in his opinion Dudek "has been downgraded ... I think that he's going to come back, and there will be a revival. People are going to pay more attention to his work. I think he was neglected chiefly because he chose to publish with the private presses. His books just haven't had the publicity. They haven't been as widely reviewed, as much as Layton's for example."

Recalling the past, he says, "I think he's got to be remembered as one of the chief poets of the 40's. He's also had a great influence as an editor and as a supporter through his publishing enterprizes. He's been a champion of Montreal poetry. He always claimed that Montreal had the best poetry – even though at times that wasn't so. Actually, I wish he'd been more of a force over the last fifteen years than he has been, as far as reputation is concerned. I wish that what he stood for was better known. His ideas and his work haven't reached a large enough public – the public he should have had."

13 June 1982
Toronto, Ontario

129

Interview with Ronald Sutherland

*Sutherland lives and writes in North Hatley, Quebec, — next door to D.G. Jones and Ralph Gustafson, just down the street from Frank Scott, and around the lake from Louis Dudek. He teaches CanLit at the University of Sherbrooke and has written, along with a few novels, two works of criticism, **Second Image** and **The New Hero**. Fluently bilingual, Sutherland has embraced as his special province the interesting dichotomy that exists between English Canadian and Québec literature.*

"   I was always favorably impressed with Louis Dudek because he was the first person who introduced me to Canadian Literature. He and Hugh MacLennan were at McGill at the time, and of course there were no Canadian Literature courses as such. I was from the East End of Montreal and came up to McGill taking a formal BA in Philosophy and English and happened to get into one of Louis Dudek's classes. He would talk about Canadian literature, and for me it was an amazing thing to find out about CanLit because in high school we hadn't ever been informed that there were people writing in our own country. Later on I came to know that Louis was not only talking about Canadian literature but producing it, and not only producing it but fostering it in many ways — in the publications, in the encouragement he gave to all the younger writers, and in the anthology which he and Layton just then brought out.

"So in a hundred ways he was one of the major fostering forces for the whole of Canadian literature in Montreal. A lot of young people would not have gotten into poetry or writing of any sort had it not been for Dudek.

"Dudek had contacts with other writers such as Ezra Pound and was able to keep the whole thing in perspective. That is to say he would never allow anybody to remain provincial for long. He kept the whole world of Canadian writing in the international context, and I think this is important, too, because he was able to apply strict international standards. He always did that. Of course, he infuriated some people, because if a Canadian poet wasn't writing good poetry Dudek would say so and point out why. I think this was important because there was always a tendency to say that just because something was Canadian it was good; but Dudek never accepted that position. He always maintained that a good Canadian poet should be judged by international standards.

"Louis influenced my life because he was the first to kindle my interest in Canadian literature. First as my professor, then later on as I got to know him on a professional basis and was able to appreciate what he had been doing, so we made contact on many occasions. I think I developed a more acute critical judgment from reading his criticism. Louis is a stimulating and provocative conversationalist. There is never any small talk between us.

"Dudek was brought up about eight blocks away from me. There was a place called the Dom Polski Hall where we used to attend dances. We've had more curious parallels than that. Dudek's real name is more complicated,* I'm in the same boat. Sutherland is not my real name either. I am, in fact a cousin to the President of Argentina.**

---

* Asked about this, Dudek said that the family name "Dudek" was adopted around the middle of the nineteenth century when a great-great-grandfather, a Polish patriot-revolutionary, took the name and identification papers of a dead Czech soldier. The original family name was something like Sierakowski. Dudek learned this story when a distant relative from Australia passed through Montreal a few years ago.

** Signor Bignone, a cousin of Ronald Sutherland, who was named Sutherland by adoption.

"I believe I was one of three students at McGill University from the East End of Montreal. It just didn't happen often in those days. I do think Louis had a special sympathy because of this. I remember dropping in and talking to him (he always seemed to have time) because we had a lot in common, we always got along well together. The first stuff I ever wrote, I took to him. Dudek and I lean toward the same kind of social realism. We share the same kind of insights, derived from realistic fiction. The short, sharp, ironical poems he writes appeal to me more than the longer poems, however.

"His leading characteristic, I think is his honest, objective criticism. He seems to be able, always, to look at things objectively. He also has a sharp critical mind. I very much enjoy his *First Person in Literature*. There's a marvellous intellectual power there, but the quality that first strikes me is the fact that he's absolutely honest. For example, he will accuse poets of sloppiness and be absolutely right, but this doesn't win friends and influence people as a rule.

"The man has never been an aggressive self-promoter. His modesty has perhaps prevented him from getting the recognition he deserves. He has always quietly worked in the background, doing his own writing, encouraging others. So he's not as widely known as he might be, but I think he is known among all serious Canadian writers and students of Canadian literature.

"In the recent anthology *Understanding Canada*, prepared for Canadian studies in the United States, I cite Dudek on several occasions, as well as his translations, in the section on Literature.

"I try to employ in my work the objective honesty he shows in his, and I try also to apply international standards in my criticism as he does. If I don't follow him exactly I certainly work along lines parallel to him.

"He definitely has to be called one of the Deans of Canadian Studies."

14 July 1982
North Hatley, Quebec

ENDNOTES

Chapter I

1. Louis Dudek, "The Literary Significance of Grove's Search," Inscape, Symposium issue, Vol. XI, No. 1, *The Grove Edition* 1974, p. 90.
2. Louis Dudek, *Epigrams* (Montreal: DC Books, 1975), p. 1.
3. Jean-Jacques Rousseau, *The Confessions* (1953; rpt. England: Penguin, 1975), p. 17.
4. Louis Dudek, *The First Person In Literature* (Toronto: CBC Publications, 1967), p. 8.
5. *Ibid.*, p. 8.

Chapter II

6. Lilian Dudek, "A personal conversation," (Montreal: December 16, 1976).
7. Lilian Dudek, "A personal conversation," (Montreal: March 7, 1977).
8. Louis Dudek, "Recorded Conversation Regarding His Poetry" (Montreal: December 10, 1975). All subsequent references to recorded conversations with Louis Dudek will follow the passage in brackets marked (RC) and the date. See Bibliography: Recorded Conversations, pp. 111-112.
9. Lilian Dudek, "A personal conversation" (Montreal: Dec. 16/76).
10. Louis Dudek, "Autobiographical Sketch Written for Ryerson Press" (Montreal: 6 Oct. 1951), Queen's University Archives: The Lorne Pierce Collection (Kingston), p. 1. (Hereafter referred to as "Autobiographical Sketch").
11. Louis Dudek, "The Loaded Gun," unpublished poem: released only for use in this work.
12. Lilian Dudek, "A personal conversation" (Montreal: Dec. 16/76).
13. Louis Dudek, "Autobriographical Sketch," p. 1.
14. *Ibid.*, pp. 1-2.

15. *Ibid.*, p. 1.

16. *Ibid.*, p. 2.

17. Louis Dudek, ed., *worlds of poetry: all kinds of everything* (Toronto/Vancouver: Clarke, Irwin, 1973), n.p.

18. Louis Dudek, "Autobriographical Sketch," p. 3.

19. Lilian Dudek, "A personal conversation" (Montreal: March 8/77).

20. Louis Dudek, "Autobiographical Sketch," p. 3.

21. Louis Dudek, "Autobiographical Sketch," pp. 2-3.

22. *Ibid.*, p. 3.

23. *Ibid.*, p. 2.

24. Louis Dudek, "Autobiographical Sketch," p. 4.

25. Michael Darling, "An Interview with Louis Dudek," *Essays on Canadian Writing*, No. 3 (Fall 1975), pp. 13-14.

26. Louis Dudek, "A Problem of Meaning," *Canadian Literature*, 59 (1974), p. 16.

27. See: Donald Creighton, *The Story of Canada*, 2nd, ed. (1959; rvd., rpt. Great Britain: MacMillan, 1971), p. 231 ff.

Chapter III

28. *McGill Daily*, 6 Oct. 1936, Vol. XXVI, No. 4.

29. *Ibid.*, 18 March 1938, Vol. XXVII, No. 99.

30. *Ibid.*, 25 May 1939, Vol. XXVIII, No. 8.

31. Louis Dudek, "Autobiographical Sketch," pp. 3-4.

32. Louis Dudek, "Life," *McGill Daily*, 21 Oct. 1937, Vol. XXVII, No. 15, p. 2, Cols. 4-5.

33. *Ibid.*, 12 Nov. 1937, Vol. XXVII, No. 30, p. 2. Col 3. See "Louis Dudek" entry in Old McGill (annual yearbook), 1939, in which he quotes as his motto: "Rightly to be great/ Is not to stir without great argument ..." He loves an intellectual argument and always had a strong argumentative bent. His favourite Platonic dialogue is the Protagoras.

34. Louis Dudek, "Autobiographical Sketch," p. 5.

35. *Ibid., loc. cit.*

36. *Ibid.*, pp. 5-6.

37. Louis Dudek, "Autobiographical Sketch," p. 6.

38. Louis Dudek, "Correspondence," *The Golden Dog*, 4 (1974), 2.

39. *Ibid., p. 1.*

40. Desmond Pacey, *Creative Writing in Canada*, 2nd ed. (1952; rpt. Toronto: Ryerson Press, 1964), p. 124.

41. *Ibid., loc. cit.*

42. *Ibid.*, p. 185.

43. *Ibid., loc. cit.*

44. Louis Dudek, "Poets of Revolt...or Reaction?" *First Statement*, 15 June 1943, Vol. 1, No. 20, p. 5.

45. *Ibid.*

46. Louis Dudek, "Geography, Politics, and Poetry," *First Statement*, 2 April 1943, Vol. 1, No. 16, p. 3.

47. Louis Dudek, "The People Like It," *First Statement*, 14 April 1943, Vol. 1, No. 15, p. 7.

48. Irving Layton, *Collected Poems, Irving Layton* (Toronto: McClelland and Stewart Ltd., 1965), p. 62.

49. Irving Layton, *Selected Poems* (Toronto: McClelland and Stewart Ltd., 1969), p. 1.

50. Raymond Souster, *The Colour of the Times* (Toronto: Ryerson Press, 1951), p. 8.

51. Louis Dudek, "Autobiographical Sketch," pp. 7-8.

Chapter IV

52. Geoffrey Chaucer, "Troilus and Criseyde": *The Works of Geoffrey Chaucer*, ed. F.N. Robinson (1933; rpt. Boston: Houghton Mifflin Co., 1961), p. 479, L. 1814-1825.

53. Dagobert D. Runes, ed., *Dictionary of Philosophy* (New York: Philosophical Library, 1960), p. 69.

54. Douglas Barbour, "Poet as Philosopher," *Canadian Literature*, No. 53 (Summer 1972), p. 19.

55. Wynne Francis, "A Critic of Life," *Canadian Literature*, No. 22 (Autumn 1964), p. 11.

56. Louis Dudek, "Autobiographical Sketch," p. 8.

58. Irving Layton, "Personal conversation," Montreal: May 21, 1976.

59. See also Ezra Pound, Cantons LXXVI, "Arachne, che me porta fortuna" (Spider that brings me luck), and "That butterfly has gone out through my smoke hole."

60. Louis Dudek, "Autobiographical Sketch," p. 8.

61. *Ibid.*, pp. 8-9.

62. *Ibid.*, p. 9.

63. *Ibid.*, p. 9.

64. *Ibid.*, p. 10.

65. *Ibid.*, p. 10.

66. Louis Dudek, "Autobiographical Sketch," p. 11.

67. Oscar Wilde, "The Picture of Dorian Gray," in *Complete Works of Oscar Wilde* (London: Collins Clear-Type Press, 1973), pp. 54-55.

68. Douglas Barbour, "Poet as Philosopher," *Canadian Literature*, No. 53 (Summer 1972), p. 21.

Chapter V

69. Louis Dudek, "Autobiographical Sketch," p. 11.

70. *Ibid, loc. cit.*

71. Frank Davey, *From There to Here*, Press Porcepic (1974), p. 93.

72. *Ibid.*, p. 92.

73. Davey, p. 93.

74. L. Dudek and M. Gnarowski, ed., *The Making of Modern Poetry in Canada* (Toronto: 1967), p. 172.

75. Louis Dudek, "The Making of *CIV/n*," in *Index to CIV/n: A Little Magazine Edited by Aileen Collins* (Quebec: Culture, 1965), pp. 3-4.

76. See Sections 39 and 40 of *Europe*.

77. Louis Dudek, "Art, Entertainment and Religion," *Queen's Quarterly*, LXX, No. 3 (Autumn 1963), p. 425.

78. L. Dudek and M. Gnarowski, ed., "The Little Magazine," *The Making of Modern Poetry in Canada* (Toronto, 1967), p. 203.

79. Irving Layton, "An Open Letter to Louis Dudek," *Cataract*, Vol. 1, No. 2 (Winter 1962), n.p.

80. Michael Darling, "An Interview with Louis Dudek," *Essays on Canadian Writing*, No. 3 (Fall 1975), p. 12.

81. L. Dudek, ed., "Editorial," *Delta* (October 1957), p. 2.

82. *Ibid.*, p. 3.

83. Frank Davey, *From There to Here*, Press Porcepic (1974), p. 93.

84. John Nause and J. Michael Heenan, "An Interview With Louis Dudek," *The Tamarack Review*, 69 (1976), p. 39.

85. Darling, "An Interview With Louis Dudek," p. 12.

86. Nause and Heenan, "An Interview with Louis Dudek," p. 33.

87. *Ibid.*, p. 39.

Chapter VI

88. Darling, "An Interview with Louis Dudek," p. 12.

89. Louis Dudek, "The Psychology of Literature," *Canadian Literature*, no. 72, (Spring 1977), p. 11.

90. Dudek, "The Psychology of Literature," p. 5.

91. *Ibid.*, p. 15.

92. Percy Bysshe Shelley, "Ode to the West Wind," *The Oxford Book of English Verse*, ed. Arthur Quiller-Couch (London: Oxford University Press, 1922), p. 709.

93. John Nause and J. Michael Heenan, "An Interview with Louis Dudek," *The Tamarack Review*, 69 (1976), p. 39.

94. *Ibid.*, pp. 40-41.

95. Michael Darling, "An Interview with Louis Dudek," *Essays on Canadian Writing*, No. 3 (fall 1975), pp. 13-14.

96. K. Esplin, ed., "An Afternoon With F. R. Scott," *Cyan Line* (Fall 1976), p. 21.

97. Louis Dudek, "The Fallacy of Literalism and the Failing of Symbolic Interpretation," *Delta*, 24 (1964), pp. 21-22.

98. Louis Dudek, "Correspondence with Dr. Lorne Pierce," The Lorne Pierce Papers, Queen's University Archives, Kingston, February 20, 1951.

99. Dorothy Livesay, "The Sculpture of Poetry," *Canadian Literature*, 30, (Autumn 1966), pp. 26-35.

100. The Dorothy Livesay Papers, Queen's University Archives, "Letters from Louis Dudek," December 17, 1965.

101. Frank Davey, *From There to Here*, Press Porcepic (1974), p. 93.

102. John Robert Colombo, "Dudek, The Last of the Lot," *The Globe and Mail*, Toronto (January 31, 1976), p. 37.

103. Louis Dudek, "The Future of French Canada," Delta, No. 23 (March 1964), p. 6.

104. Dudek, "The Future of French Canada," p. 6.

105. Louis Dudek, "Patates au Four," *McGill Daily*, Jan. 15, 1943.

106. Louis Dudek, "Les Innocents," *Northern Review*, Vol. 4 (Jan-Feb 1949).

107. Louis Dudek, "Advanced French," *Contact*, No. 1 (Jan. 1952).

108. Emile Nelligan, "Soir d'Hiver," *First Statement*, 2, No. 3 (Oct. 1943), p. 18; "Claire de Lune Intellectuel," *First Statement*, 2, No. 3 (Oct. 1943), pp. 18-19; "Serenade Triste," *First Statement*, 2, No. 3 (Oct, 1943), p. 19.

109. Louis Dudek, "The Future of French Canada," *Delta*, No 23 (mar. 1964); "Parenté des Littérature française et anglaise au Canada," *Lettres et Écritures*, Vol. 1, No. 2 (Feb. 1964); "The Future of Culture in Quebec," *Gazette* (Feb. 19, 1966); "Translations Enrich French-English Literature," *Gazette* (May 21, 1966), p. 19.

Chapter VII

110. Ezra Pound, *The Cantos of Ezra Pound* (New York: James Laughlin, 1948), p. 437.

111. John Robert Colombo, "Dudek, The Last of the Lot," *The Globe and Mail*, Toronto, Jan. 31, 1976, p. 37.

112. John Nause and J, Michael Heenan, "An Interview with Louis Dudek," *The Tamarack Review*, 69 (1976), pp. 39-40.

113. Nause and Heenan, "An Interview ...," p. 42.

114. Nause and Heenan, "An Interview ...," p. 43.

115. Frank Davey, *From There to Here*, Press Porcepic (1974), p. 95.

116. Michael Darling, "An Interview with Louis Dudek," *Essays on Canadian Writing*, No. 3 (Fall 1975), pp. 2-3.

SELECTED BIBLIOGRAPHY

Primary Sources

Dudek, Louis. *East of the city*. Toronto: Ryerson Press, 1946.

_____ *The Searching Image*. Toronto: Ryerson Press, 1952.

_____ *Cerberus*. Toronto: Contact Press, 1952.

_____ *Twenty-Four Poems*. Toronto: Contact Press, 1952.

_____ *Europe*. Toronto: Laocoon (Contact) Press, 1956.

_____ *The Transparent Sea*. Toronto: Contact Press, 1956.

_____ *En Mexico*. Toronto: Contact Press, 1958.

_____ *Laughing Stalks*. Toronto: Contact Press, 1958.

_____ *Atlantis*. Montreal: Delta (Canada), 1967.

_____ *Collected Poetry*. Montreal: Delta Canada, 1971.

_____ *Epigrams*. Montreal: DC Books, 1975.

_____ "Continuation 1." *The Tamarack Review*. No. 69. Toronto: The University of Toronto Press, Summer 1976.

_____ *Technology and Culture: Six Lectures*. Ottawa: The Golden Dog Press, 1979.

_____ *Cross-Section: Poems 1940-1980*. Toronto: The Coach House Press, 1980.

_____ *Continuation 1*. Montreal: Vehicule Press, 1981.

_____ *Poems From Atlantis*. Ottawa: The Golden Dog Press, 1981.

141

Dudek, Louis. "Unpublished Autobiographical Sketch" /Written for Ryerson Press, Montreal: 6 October 1951. Released only by written permission from Louis Dudek/. Queen's University Archives: The Lorne Pierce Collection. Kingston, Ontario.

_____ *Ideas for Poetry.* Montreal: Véhicule Press, 1983.

_____ "Louis Dudek Issue." *Open Letter.* Toronto: Spring and Summer, 1981.

Recorded Conversations with Louis Dudek

Louis Dudek. Tape 1: *East of the City, The Transparent Sea.* 16 Oct. 1975, 90 Minutes.

_____ Tape 2: *The Transparent Sea.* 16 Oct. 1975. 90 minutes.

_____ Tape 3: *Europe.* 5 Nov. 1975, 90 minutes.

_____ Tape 4: *Laughing Stalks.* 13 Nov. 1975, 60 minutes.

_____ Tape 5: *Europe.* 5 Nov. 1975, pp. 100-139.
En Mexico, 13 Nov. 1975, 90 minutes.

_____ Tape 6: *Atlantis.* 10 Dec. 1975, pp. 1-6, 60 minutes.
(Voices garbled).

_____ Tape 7: *Atlantis.* 10 Dec 1975, pp. 11-36, 60 minutes.

_____ Tape 8: *Atlantis.* 10 Dec. 1975, pp. 39-56, 60 minutes.

_____ Tape 9: *Atlantis.* 10 Dec. 1975, pp. 58-83, 60 minutes.

_____ Tape 10: Atlantis, pp. 83-93, *Cerberus, 24 Poems.* 10 Dec. 1975, 60 minutes.

_____ Tape 11: *Atlantis*, pp. 93-130, 23 Sept. 1976, 60 minutes.

_____ Tape 12: *Atlantis*, pp. 132-149, *Collected Poetry*, pp. 218-294. 30 Sept. 1976, 90 minutes.

_____ Tape 13: *Collected Poetry*, pp. 295-323. 23 Sept. 1976, 90 minutes.

_____ Tape 14: *Collected Poetry*, p. 323. 4 Oct. 1976; "Conversation," 30 Nov. 1976, 90 minutes.

_____ Tape 15: *Collected Poetry.* 30 Nov. 1976, 90 minutes.

NOTE: There are occasional pages of Atlantis that have not been discussed during recorded conversations. Poems having no biographical relevance are not mentioned in this series of recordings. The tapes are presently in the possession of the author.

Correspondence

Alan Crawley Papers (1951-1966). Queen's University Archives, Kingston.

Ralph Gustafson Papers (1965-1966). Queen's University Archives, Kingston.

Dorothy Livesay Papers (1952-1966). Queen's University Archives, Kingston.

Al Purdy Papers (1969). Queen's University Archives, Kingston.

Literary Criticism

Dudek, Louis. "Life." *McGill Daily*, 27, No. 15 (21 Oct. 1937), p. 2 and No. 30 (12 Nov. 1937), p. 3.

——————— "The People Like It." (poem). *First Statement*, 15 (March 1943), p. 7.

——————— Geography, Politics, and Poetry." *First Statement*, 1, No. 16 (April 1943), p. 2.

——————— "Poets of Revolt... or Reaction?" *First Statement*, 1, No. 20 (June 1943), p. 5.

——————— "Academic Literature." *First Statement*, 2, No. 8 (August 1944), pp. 17-29.

——————— "Editorial." *Delta* (October 1957), p. 2.

——————— "The Role of Little Magazines in Canada," *Canadian Forum*, 38 (July 1958), pp. 76-78.

——————— "Art, Entertainment and Religion." *Queen's Quarterly*, 70 (Autumn 1963), pp. 413-430.

——————— "The Future of French Canada." *Delta*, No. 23 (March 1964), p. 6.

——————— "The Fallacy of Literalism and the Failing of Symbolic Interpretation." *Delta*, 24 (1964), pp. 21-22.

——————— "The Making of *CIV/n*" *Index to CIV/n* (1965), pp. 3-4.

——————— "A Problem of Meaning." *Canadian Literature*, No. 59 (1974), p. 16.

——————— "Correspondence." *The Golden Dog*, No. 4 (1974), p. 2.

——————— "The Psychology of Literature." *Canadian Literature*, No. 72 (Spring 1977), pp. 5-20.

——————— "The Poetic Life (If There Is One)". *Scrivener* (Spring, 1982), p. 12-13.

Dudek, Louis and Michael Gnarowski, ed. "The Little Magazine." *The Making of Modern Poetry in Canada*. Toronto: Ryerson Press (1967), p. 203.

Studies

Dudek, Louis. *Literature and the Press:* A History of Printing, Printed Media, and Their Relation to Literature. Toronto: Ryerson/Contact Press, 1960.

_____ *The First Person in Literature.* Toronto: CBC Publications, 1967.

_____ *Dk/Some Letters of Ezra Pound.* Montreal: DC Books, 1974.

_____ *Technology and Culture: Six Lectures.* Ottawa: The Golden Dog Press, 1979.

_____ *Selected Essays and Criticism.* Ottawa: The Tecumseh Press Limited, 1978.

SECONDARY LITERATURE

Biographical

The Canadian Who's Who. Vol. 12. Toronto: Who's Who Canadian Publications, 1972, pp. 303-304.

Creative Canada: A Biographical Dictionary of Twentieth-Century Creative and Performing Artists. (Compiled by the Reference Division of the McPherson Library, University of Victoria.) Vol. 2, Toronto: University of Toronto Press, 1972, p. 82.

Davey, Frank. *From There to Here: A Guide to English-Canadian Literature Since 1960, Our Nature – Our Voices*, Vol. II. Erin: Press Porcepic, 1974, pp. 92-97.

Davey, Frank. *Louis Dudek and Raymond Souster*. Studies in Canadian Literature. Douglas and McIntyre: Vancouver, 1980.

Dudek, Lilian. "Personal Conversation." Montreal (16 Dec. 1976, 8 March 1977).

Gustafson, Ralph. *Contemporary Poets of the English Language*. Ed. by Rosalie Murphy. Chicago/London: St. James Press, 1970, pp. 308-310.

Story, Norah. *The Oxford Companion to Canadian History and Literature*. Toronto: Oxford University Press, 1967, p. 229.

Sylvestre, Guy, Brandon Conron, and Carl F. Klinck, eds. *Canadian Writers/Écrivains Canadiens*. Revised Edition, Toronto: Ryerson Press, 1967, pp. 42-43.

Toye, William, ed. *Supplement to the Oxford Companion to Canadian History and Literature*. Toronto: Oxford University Press, 1973, pp. 70-71.

Weaver, Robert and William Toye, eds. *The Oxford Anthology of Canadian Literature*. Toronto: Oxford University Press, 1973, pp. 113-114.

Wenek, Karol. *Louis Dudek: A Check List*. Ottawa, 1975, pp. 44-45*

---

* New reference material has been added to Wenek's Check-List and material not relevant to this study has been deleted.

Criticism

Adams, Percy. Letter to the Editor re "The Paperback Revolution ..." *Delta*, No. 15 (Aug. 1961), p. 28.

Adams, Rich. "Louis Dudek: Mind over Matter." *It Needs to be Said* (Louis Dudek issue), No. 4 (Autumn 1974), p. 2.

Barbour, Douglas. "Poet as Philosopher." *Canadian Literature*, No. 53 (Summer 1972), pp. 18-29.

Boxer, Avi. "Où sont les jeunes?" (Poem.) *CIV/n*, No. 1 (Winter 1953), p. 8.

Colombo, John Robert. "Dudek: The Last of the Lot." *The Globe and Mail*. Toronto (31 Jan. 1976), p. 37.

Corman, Cid. "Another Letter on Poetry and Myth." *Delta*, No. 7 (April 1959), p. 4.

Darling, Michael. "An Interview with Louis Dudek." *Essays on Canadian Writing*, No. 3 (Fall 1975), pp. 2-14.

Ellenbogen, George. "An Open Letter to Irving Layton." *Cataract*, 1, No. 3 (July 1962), n.p.

Eigner, Larry. "Obscenity, Civilization, Literature & Forests." *Delta*, No. 10 (Jan.-Mar. 1960), p. 19.

Extracts from Dudek Letters. "Functional Poetry Etc." *Delta*, No. 9 (Oct.-Dec. 1959), pp. 11-13.

Francis, Wynne. "Montreal Poets of the Forties." *Canadian Literature*, (February 1978).

_____. "Little Magazines and Small Presses," *The Laurentian Review*, (February 1978).

_____. "A Critic of Life: Louis Dudek as Man of Letters." *Canadian Literature*, No. 22 (Autumn 1964), pp. 5-23.

Gnarowski, Michael. "Of Prophets and Multiple Visions." *Yes*, No. 13 (Dec. 1964), pp. 1-3.

_____. "Louis Dudek: A Note." *Yes*, No. 14 (Sept. 1965), n.p.

146

Gnarowski, Michael, Glen Siebrasse. "Editorial." (Reply to an unpublished letter from Louis Dudek). *Yes*, 1, No. 3 (Dec, 1956), n.p.

Goldie, Terry. "Louis Dudek: First Person on Literature." *It Needs to be Said* (Louis Dudek Issue), No. 4 (Autumn 1974), pp. 7-8.

Gustafson, Ralph. Letter to the Editor re "Vs. the Literature of Pessimism ... (sic)." *Delta*, No. 16 (Nov. 1961), p. 8.

Heenan, Michael. "The voice of Order in Louis Dudek's Collected Poetry." *Inscape*, II, No. 2 (Spring 1974), pp. 41-47.

Jones, Douglas G. "A Letter on Poetry and Belief." *Delta*, No. 3 (April 1958), pp. 17-20. (Reply by Dudek, p. 32.)

Layton, Irving. "Letter to Louis Dudek." (Poem). *Contact*, 2, No. 2 (Feb.-Apr. 1953), p. 9.

_____. "An Open Letter to Louis Dudek." *Cataract*, 1, No. 2 (Winter 1962), n.p.

_____. "Personal Conversation." Montreal (31 May 1976).

Livesay, Dorothy. "The Sculpture of Poetry: On Louis Dudek." *Canadian Literature*, No. 30 (Autumn 1966), pp. 26-35.

Nause, John and J, Michael Heenan. "An Interview with Louis Dudek." *The Tamarack Review*, No. 69 (1976), pp. 30-44.

Pacey, Desmond. "Modern Canadian Poetry." *Creative Writing in Canada*. Revised edition, Toronto: Ryerson Press, 1961, pp. 170-174.

Pound, Ezra. "Ezra Pound: A Letter." *Delta*, No. 8 (July 1959), p. 17.

Purdy, Al. Untitled note on Dudek. *Moment*, No. 1 (1960), p. 6.

_____. "Mexico as Seen by Looie the Lip." (Poem.) *Moment*, No. 1 (1960), p. 8.

_____. "Dudek's Crazy Theory Refuted (or proven maybe)." (Poem). *Delta*, No. 15 (Aug. 1961), pp. 22-23.

Richmond, John. "Purposeful Poet." *Start Supp*. Montreal (6 Nov. 1971), p. B3.

Sicle, John Van. "A Critical Letter." *Delta*, No. 14 (March 1961), pp. 11-12. (Reply by Dudek, p. 13).

Smith, Arthur James Marshall. *Letter to the Editor* re "Vs. the Literature of Pessimism ..." *Delta*, No. 16 (Nov. 1961), p. 3.

Souster, Raymond. "'Où sont les jeunes?: A Reply to Louis Dudek." (Preface in the form of an open letter). *Poets 56: Ten Younger English-Canadians*. Toronto: Contact Press, 1956, n.p.

Sutherland, John. "Three New Poets." *First Statement*, 1 No. 12 (Feb. 1943), pp. 1-4.

Wenek, Karol. "Louis Dudek: The Metamorphoses." *It Needs To Be Said* (Louis Dudek Issue), No. 4 (Autumn 1974), pp. 6-7.

Reviews

Unit of Five. Toronto: Ryerson Press, 1946.
Brown, E.K. *University of Toronto Quarterly*, 14. (April 1945), p. 264.
Frye, Northrop. *Canadian Forum*, 25 (May 1945), p. 48. Sutherland, John.
First Statement, 2, No. 11, (Feb.-Mar. 1945), pp. 30-31.

East of the City. Toronto: Ryerson Press: 1946.
Birney, Earle. *Canadian Poetry*, 10 (Dec. 1946), pp. 43-47.
Brown, E.K. *University of Toronto Quarterly*, 16 (April 1947), p. 251.
Smith, A.J.M. *Canadian Forum*, 27 (May 1948), pp. 42-43.

The Searching Image. Toronto: Ryerson Press, 1952.
Frye, Northrop. *University of Toronto Quarterly*, 22 (April 1953),
pp. 278-279.

Twenty-Four Poems. Toronto: Contact Press, 1952.
Frye, Northrop. *University of Toronto Quarterly*, 22 (April 1953), p. 278.

Cerberus. Toronto: Contact Press, 1952.
Compton, Neil. *CIV/n*, No. 2 (Spring 1953), pp. 21-22.
Frye, Northrop. *University of Toronto Quarterly*, 22 (April 1953), p. 279.

Europe. Toronto: Laocoon (Contact) press, 1954.
Wilson, Milton. *Canadian Forum*, 35 (Oct. 1955),
Wilson, Milton. (Correspondence and replies. Includes letter from Dudek
under pseudonym of Alexander St.-John Swift), *Canadian Forum*, 35
(Nov. 1955), pp. 182-184.

The Transparent Sea. Toronto: Contact Press, 1956.
Dobbs, Kildare R. E. *Canadian Forum*, 36 (Jan. 1957), p. 238.
Duncan, Chester. *Tamarack Review*, No. 3 (Spring 1957), pp. 82-83.
Gnarowski, Michael, *Yes*, 1, No. 3 (Dec. 1956), n.p.

Delta. Montreal, Oct. 1957-Oct. 1966.
Birney, Earle. (Text of a talk for CBC Anthology, 29 April, 1958).
Fiddlehead, No. 36 (Spring 1958), supplement.
Extracts from letters to the Editor. *Delta*, No. 2 (Jan. 1958), pp. 28-29.

En Mexico. Toronto: Contact Press, 1958.
Pacey, Desmond. *Fiddlehead*, No. 40 (Spring 1959), pp. 50-51.
Purdy, A. W. *Canadian Forum*, 38 (Nov. 1958), pp. 187-188.

Laughing Stalks. Toronto: Contact Press, 1958.
Pacey, Desmond. *Fiddlehead*, No. 40 (Spring 1959), pp. 50-51.
Purdy, A. W. *Canadian Forum*, 38 (Nov. 1958), p. 187.

Literature and the Press. Toronto: Ryerson Press, 1960.
  Axford, H. M. (Poem). *Delta*, No. 22 (Oct. 1963), pp. 35-36.
  Emery, Tony. *Canadian Literature*, No. 9 (Summer 1961) pp. 62-64.
  McLuhan, Marshall. *University of Toronto Quarterly*, pp. 420-421.

Altantis, Montreal: Delta (Canada), 1967.
  Gasparini, Len. *Queen's Quarterly*, 75 (Autumn 1968), pp. 538-539.
  MacCallum, Hugh. *University of Toronto Quarterly*, 37 (July 1968),
    pp. 370-371
  Stevens, Peter. *Canadian Literature*, No. 39 (Winter 1969), pp. 77-78.

Collected Poetry. Montreal: Delta (Canada), 1971.
  Hornyansky, Michael. *University of Toronto Quarterly*, 41 (Summer 1972),
    pp. 332-333.
  Lee, Dennis. *Books in Canada*, 1. No. 3 (1972), pp. 14/19-20.
  Levenson, Christopher. *Queen's Quarterly*, 79 (Summer 1972), p. 274.

Dk/Some Letters of Ezra Pound. Montreal: DC Books, 1974. Fetherling,
  Douglas. *Saturday Night*, Vol. 90, No. 4 (Sept. 1975), pp. 69-75.

Epigrams. Montreal: DC Books, 1975.
  Garebian, Keith. *The Gazette*. Montreal (20 Dec. 1975), p. 53.

Cross-Section: Poems 1940-1980. Toronto: The Coach House Press, 1980.
  Stromberg-Stein, Susan. *The Gazette*. Montreal (24 Jan. 1981) p. 107.

Poems from Atlantis, Golden Dog Press; *Continuation 1*, Vehicule Press;
  Louis Dudek: Open Letter, Fourth Series, 1981. Norris, Ken. *The Gazette*.
  Montreal (13 March 1982), p. D9.

Additional Sources

Chaucer, Geoffrey. "Troilus and Criseyde." *The Works of Geoffrey Chaucer*.
  Ed. F.N. Robinson. 2nd ed. Boston: Houghton Mifflin Co., 1961.

Creighton, Donald. *The Story of Canada*. 2nd ed. 1959; rpt. Great Britain:
  McMillan, 1971.

Dictionary of Philosophy. Ed. Dagobert D. Runes. 15th ed. New York:
  Philosophical LIbrary, Inc. 1960.

Layton, Irving. *Collected Poems, Irving Layton*. Toronto: McClelland and
  Stewart, 1969.

_____. *Selected Poems*. Toronto: McClelland and Stewart, 1969.

Livesay, Dorothy. "The Sculpture of Poetry." *Canadian Literature*, 30
  (Autumn 1966), pp. 26-35.

Pacey, Desmond. *Creative Writing in Canada*. 2nd ed. 1952; rpt. Toronto:
  Ryerson Press, 1964.

Pound, Ezra. *The Cantos of Ezra Pound*. New York: James Laughlin, 1942.

Rousseau, Jean-Jacques. *The Confessions*. 2nd ed. 1953; rpt. Great Britain: Penguin Books, 1975.

Scott, Frank R. "An Afternoon with F. R. Scott." *Cyan Line*. Ed. K. Esplin. Montreal: Vehicule Press (Fall 1976), pp. 11-21.

Shelley, Percy Bysshe. "Ode to the West Wind." *The Oxford Book of English Verse*. Ed. A. Quiller-Couch. Oxford: Oxford University Press, 1922.

Souster, Raymond. *The Colour of the Times*. Toronto: Ryerson Press, 1951.

Wilde, Oscar. "The Picture of Dorian Gray." *Complete Works of Oscar Wilde*. 2nd. ed. 1966; rpt. Great Britain: Collins Clear-Type Press, 1973.

Wordsworth, William. "The Prelude." *Tradition and Revolt: The World in Literature: 3*. Ed. A. Warnock and S. Foresman. Toronto: W. J. Gage and Co. Ltd., 1951.

Worlds of Poetry: All kinds of everything. Ed. Louis Dudek. Toronto/Vancouver: Clarke Irwin, 1973.